The Garden of Eden Raw Fruit & Vegetable Recipes

by
Phyllis Avery

Hygeia Publishing Co.
1358 Fern Place, Vista, California 92083

The Garden of Eden Raw Fruit & Vegetable Recipes

ISBN 1-880598-24-8
Avery, Phyllis, 1936-
The Garden of Eden Raw Fruit & Vegetable Recipes

Other books by Phyllis Avery
Stop Your Tinnitus: Causes, Preventatives, and Treatments
100 Raw Fruit & Vegetable Recipes
The 10-Minute Vegetarian Cook Book

PUBLISHED BY:

HYGEIA PUBLISHING COMPANY
1358 Fern Place
Vista, California 92083

Cover designed by: Alonna L. Farrar, A. Boyd-Farrar Graphics, Vista, California
Typesetting by Kati Bower, Alpha & Omega Typesetting, Oceanside, California

Printed in the United States of America

TABLE OF CONTENTS

FRUIT DISHES

FRUIT SYRUPS

INTRODUCTION

Why Should We Eat Raw Foods?

There are three conditions that food should meet: it should produce mental clarity; it should not burden the body with toxins; and it should be able to be digested quickly without wasting a lot of energy. Foods that are not natural to the body—flesh, milk and milk products, and most grains—create a restlessness in the mind and body. Toxic bodies develop into an array of diseases.

Food from animals is already dead. Anything dead will begin to decompose immediately. To demonstrate this, take a cooked and uncooked apple. The cooked apple would have to be eaten immediately or be refrigerated because it has started to decay. When the cooked apple is eaten, the body is attempting to digest food that is in the process of decomposing. When the raw apple is eaten, it is being digested and assimilated in its live state.

Also, meals should be prepared and brought to the dining table with a minimum amount of time and expense.

The highest quality foods are natural, raw foods. All the nutrients are found intact. The amino acids are in their finest form. The minerals, vitamins, carbohydrates, fatty acids, trace elements and "life force" are present.

Not only do raw foods contain all the nutrients necessary for good health, growth, maintenance and repair, they do not cause or support degenerative diseases.

The heat of cooking destroys the enzymes contained in food. Because those enzymes are inactive, the body must produce its own enzymes to digest the food. Over time, that process taxes the body's ability to produce not only digestive enzymes but also enzymes needed for other biochemical reactions, leaving it weakened and vulnerable to disease.

Recent research suggests raw foods may play a role in lowering high blood pressure. In a 1986 study published in the <u>Southern Medical Journal</u>, Dr. John M. Douglass found that a diet containing between 40 and 63 percent raw foods (fruits, vegetables, seeds and seed oil, nuts, berries and raw milk) helped 32 patients lose weight and control their hypertension.

A vast quantity of existing evidence shows that a predominantly raw diet can reverse bodily degeneration which accompanies long term illness, retards the rate at which you age, bring you seemingly boundless energy, requires less sleep, and even improve your emotional outlook. Raw foods provide more body energy because much less energy is wasted eliminating the toxins developed in cooked foods.

All of these improvements are possible because raw fruits and vegetables are two to three times more efficiently utilized by the body than cooked foods. Depending on the length of time and the amount of heat used to cook food, a small amount or all of their protein, minerals, vitamin, and enzymes are destroyed.

Proteins are coagulated and the amino acids are demineralized and toxins are created in the alteration. Calcium becomes disassociated with organic compounds, and thus becomes unusable to the body. Sugars are caramelized and disorganized. Fats are disorganized and are rendered carcinogenic. Cooked fats are chemically altered into fatty acids which are not usable by the body, consequently becoming "free-floating poisons." The cooking of fats also cause them to become "saturated," which then are attracted to the linings of artery walls, where they attach and harden. The result is hardening of the arteries.

Enzymes are totally destroyed when the cooking temperature reaches 120 degrees. enzymes play a vital role in changing carbohydrates, proteins, and fats through the digestive process. The body uses these substances to provide energy, and to rebuild cells. Enzymes are essential for tissue building, blood replacement, and the release of chemical energy for muscle movement. In essence, they are the 'agents of life.' This is what is meant by "live food."

All food contains living cells in the raw state. If heat is applied to these cells, their proteins are coagulated, just the same as the white of an egg is coagulated when it is cooked. If you cooked your food sufficiently to destroy each and every one of these live cells, and tried to live on it, you would die, just the same as if you had not eaten at all. Fortunately, most persons eat fresh fruits and raw salads and food that is not thoroughly cooked, hence they are enabled to procure from the food sufficient nutrients to allow them to lead a less than optimum existence.

In quite a short time a predominantly raw diet does several things. The body's eliminative facilities can expel accumulated wastes and toxins. Optimal sodium/potassium and acid/alkaline balance are restored. Raw foods increase the micro-electric potential of cells, improving the body's use of oxygen so that both muscles and brain are energized.

When most of your food is eaten raw, you'll eat less! A raw diet affords quick satiety on less foods, hence, does not overstimulate the digestive system causing you to overeat. Raw foods are easily digested (24 hours compared to 48 to 100 hours for cooked foods). Raw foods not only restore the natural appestat (appetite control) but they help the body to achieve a normal weight. Obesity disappears steadily, painlessly, effortlessly.

Raw Versus Cooked

There is disagreement among natural hygienists as to whether certain foods should be cooked or eaten raw. Some hygienists believe cooking these particular foods releases their natural sugar content making them more digestible. The foods in question are: cauliflower, asparagus, eggplant, potatoes and other tubers. These foods are presented in the recipe book both raw and lightly steamed but raw vegetables always dominate the meal.

But Where Do I Get My Protein?

Proteins are in every living food. You can't find a single living food that doesn't have protein. Our illnesses are caused not by lack of protein but by excess of proteins. Proteins in excess of bodily needs putrefy, especially when proteins are cooked, deranging them beyond usability.

Where Do I Get Vitamin B-12?

Some people believe vegetarians are deficient in B-12 as a result of eating fruits and vegetables exclusively, but almost no natural food in nature has vitamin B-12 in it. There is no vitamin B-12 in grass either, yet cattle have plenty of vitamin B-12. We humans get our Vitamin B-12 the same way other animals do – from by-products of bacterial activity in our intestinal tract. Also certain other B complex vitamins are created in and absorbed from the intestinal tract.

What To Expect When You Improve Your Diet

Remarkable things begin to happen to the body and mind when you improve your diet. The amazing intelligence present in every cell of the body is heightened. The rule may be stated thusly: when the quality of food coming into the body is of higher quality than the elements present in body tissues, the body begins to discard the lower-grade materials to make room for the superior materials which it uses to make new and healthier tissue.

"Withdrawal" Symptoms Follow Use of Improved Diet

What are the symptoms or signs which become evident when we first begin to omit the lower-grade foods and introduce superior foods Example: when the use of a toxic stimulant such as coffee, tea, chocolate or cocoa is stopped, headaches are common and a letdown occurs. This is due to the discarding by the body of the toxins caffeine and theobromine, which are removed from the tissues and transported through the bloodstream to the eliminating organs. When the blood circulates through the brain during its many bodily rounds before the noxious agents reach their final destination for elimination, these irritants register in our consciousness as pain. Other signs of body detoxification are discomfort in the back due to the concentration of toxic materials there.

Therefore, should one wish to avoid uncomfortable symptoms, raw foods should be introduced into the diet slowly. Start by replacing one of your normal meals each day with a raw one. Drinking fresh-squeezed orange juice in the morning will give you a natural mental high lasting several hours. Gradually eliminate meat and processed foods from your diet until you reach a balance of about 75 percent raw and 25 percent cooked. At this point you will discover the benefits of raw food.

PROPER FOOD COMBINING

Food combining refers to the best combinations of foods to eat together at the same meal. Foods of differing digestive characteristics require different body enzymes and secretions for digestion. For example, nuts and seeds, which are protein foods, require an acid environment for their digestion. Starches require an alkaline environment. Fruits create an alkaline condition in the stomach, The stomach cannot possibly be acid and alkaline at the same time. Therefore, fruits and nuts should not be eaten at the same meal.

Eating foods with differing digestive times causes the fast digesting foods to be held up, resulting in fermentation. Also, if a protein is eaten with a carbohydrate, such as meat with bread or potato, the different digestive juices in contact with each other will nullify the digestion of each so that indigestion occurs.

The protein will putrefy and the carbohydrate will ferment. The result is gas and flatulence in the system with little value derived from the foods. Also, eating fruits after a regular meal guarantees fermentation.

That which is not digested only wastes the body's energy in passing it through the alimentary canal. Worse than this, the undigested food becomes soil for bacteria to feed upon, resulting in putrefaction and fermentation which irritate and poison our tissues.

This is not to say that applying the principles of food combining will insure good digestion, as there are other factors which reduce our digestive capabilities, such as eating under stressful conditions, when fatigued, before or after strenuous exercise, when feverish, during strong emotional experiences, and overeating. In addition, the use of condiments, especially salt, vinegar, alcohol, coffee, carbonated drinks, or tea during a meal retards digestion considerably. Indigestion and flatulence are also caused by swallowing air when eating too fast. All of these circumstances must be considered if one desires good digestion.

Incompatible Combinations

The following combinations of foods are the least compatible with the human digestive system. Although these combinations are commonly eaten because the eater experiences no immediate adverse reaction, the cumulative adverse effects will surface later on in life. When symptoms of indigestion do occur, many sufferers administer an antacid remedy, which neutralizes the digestive acids in the stomach. Continued use of antacids can ulcerate the stomach.

Acid/Starch Combination

All acids destroy salivary amylase, the starch-splitting enzyme in the saliva, and thus arrest starch digestion in the mouth and stomach. Additionally, due to the differing transit times of fruits and starches, the fruits will be detained in the stomach, resulting in fermentation.

Protein/Starch Combination

As stated earlier, salivary amylase is destroyed in the stomach in the presence of a highly acidic medium. Since protein digestion requires such a medium, this combination is unacceptable.

Protein/Protein Combination

Each type of protein food requires different timing and different modifications of the digestive secretions. When one protein is combined with another protein, digestion becomes difficult. As protein is the most difficult food nutrient for the body to digest, it would beneficial to consume only one type of protein at a meal. This would not exclude the eating of two or more types of nuts at a meal, as their composition is relatively similar. (Note: The most recent data concerning protein needs has shown that it is unnecessary to consume all essential amino acids at each meal).

Acid/Protein Combination

The enzyme pepsin will only be active in the presence of one particular acid, hydrochloric acid. Other acids may actually destroy this enzyme, including fruit acids.

There is an exception to this rule. The proteins such as nuts, seeds, and cheese, do not decompose as rapidly as other proteins, due to their high fat content. The inhibiting effect of fat on the gastric digestion of protein causes these types of proteins to receive their strongest digestive juice during the latter part of digestion. Therefore, the fruit acids do not delay the secretion of gastric juice any more than the fat content of these particular proteins. These circumstances make it acceptable to eat acid fruits with nuts, or cheese.

Fat/protein Combination

Fats inhibit the flow of gastric juice, interfering with protein digestion. Since our need for fat is very little, and most protein foods already contain sufficient quantity of fat, any additional fat intake becomes difficult to digest. Avoid combining butter, oils, avocado, etc. with protein foods.

Sugar/Protein Combination

Sugars also inhibit the secretion of gastric juice interfering with protein digestion. This is true of both fruit sugars and commercial sugars.

Sugar/Starch Combination

If starch is combined with sugar, the starch is disguised, preventing the adaptation of the saliva to starch digestion. Eating fruit-filled pastry and the mixing of juice and/or fruits with cereals or breads produces indigestion, and therefore prevents the body from assimilating food.

Take Milk Alone

Milk and milk products are difficult to digest in themselves, thus making them impossible to combine with other foods. Combining milk and fruit is worse than combining milk with meat or vegetables because fruit takes much less time to digest than any other food. The fruit is held up in the stomach awaiting the more lengthy digestive time required by the milk. If you absolutely must consume milk and milk products, consume them alone. Since their indigestibility causes putrefaction and fermentation in the digestive tract, at least you won't be destroying other foods.

Melons

Melons decompose faster than other fruits. For this reason it's best to eat melons alone, or leave them alone.

Avocado

The avocado provides us with an excellent, natural source of fat. It combines best with non-starch vegetables and makes a fair combination with acid fruits.

Nuts & Seeds

Concentrated foods such as nuts and seeds should be eaten with, or as part of, a vegetable salad. The water content of the salad vegetables offsets the lack of water in nuts and seeds.

Tomatoes

The tomato, although generally thought to be a vegetable, is really an acid fruit. Due to its low sugar content, it may be combined with non-starchy vegetables. Tomatoes would not be combined with either starches or proteins, except nuts, seeds, and avocados.

Lettuce & Celery with Fruits

Fruits, except melons, may be combined with either lettuce or celery, as these vegetables are neutral in digestion, they enhance digestion of the fruits, especially the concentrated, sweet varieties.

Juices

Juice is a concentrated food, and should be considered as an entire meal. When drinking fruit or vegetable juice, drink them about 20 minutes before a meal, since they dilute the digestive secretions.

Proper Food Combining & the Recipes in This Book

In trying to offer a variety of dishes, some of the recipes are not combined according to the laws of natural food combining. Those recipes are ones with fruit and nuts combined, and starchy vegetables with nuts. There are only two vegetable and fruit combinations, and they are the Stuffed Grape Leaves recipe and the Carrot & Apple Salad.

If you are inclined to suffer from indigestion, I suggest you avoid these recipes. There are very few of them in the book. Not everyone will have a noticeable effect from eating these improper combinations but no one will get the full value from the foods.

Acid-Forming Foods

All dairy products are acid-forming except butter which is neutral. Likewise with all animal products. All grains and grain products excepting millet. Virtually all legumes, especially lentils, peanuts and most beans are acid in metabolic reaction. Chickpeas are only mildly acid-forming.

Alkaline-Forming Foods

All vegetables including sprouts, except asparagus are alkaline forming. All fruits except blueberries and olives are alkalineforming. Nuts excepting almonds and chestnuts are acid-forming. Most seeds, notably sunflower, sesame and pumpkin are alkaline forming. Also, alkaline in reaction are certain beans such as soybeans, lima beans, peas and snap beans and fresh young corn still in a sweet condition.

Behold! I have given you ever herb yielding seed, Which is upon the face of all the earth, and every tree, in which is the fruit of a tree yielding seed...To you, it shall be for food. God-In the Beginning

It is my view that the vegetarian manner of living, by its purely physical effect on the human temperament, would most beneficially influence the lot of mankind. Albert Einstein, 1940.

FOOD COMBINING CHART FOR COMPLETE AND EFFICIENT DIGESTION

☆ PROTEINS AND STARCHES EATEN TOGETHER TEND TO SPOIL IN THE STOMACH ☆

POOR
INDIGESTION • WEIGHT GAIN • FATIGUE

PROTEINS
(CONCENTRATED FOODS)

Bean sprouts	*Meat
*Cheese	*Milk
Coconut	Nuts (raw)
Dried beans	Nut butters
Dried peas	Seeds
*Eggs	Seed butters
*Fish	Soybeans
*Fowl	Sunflower sprouts
Garbanzo beans	Tofu
Lentils	*Yogurt

Not recommended, but included for clarity.

← POOR →

FATS

Avocado	Olives
Butter	*Margarine
Cream	Sour Cream
*Lard	

OILS

Avocado	Sunflower
Corn	Sesame
Nut	Soy
Olive	Safflower

← GOOD →

STARCHES
(CONCENTRATED FOODS)

Artichokes	Parsnips
Beets	Pasta
Carrots	Peas
Chestnuts	Potatoes
Coconuts	Pumpkins
Grains	Split peas
Lentils	Turnips
Lima beans	Winter squash
Mature corn	Yams

GOOD (left)

GOOD ↕

GOOD (right)

NON-STARCHY VEGETABLES
(HIGH WATER CONTENT FOODS)

Asparagus	Collards	Kale	Summer squashes
Beet greens	Crookneck squash	Kohlrabi	Sweet pepper
Broccoli	Cucumber	Lettuce	Tomatoes
Brussels sprouts	Dandelion	Okra	Turnips
Cabbage	Eggplant	Parsley	Water cress
Celery	Endive	Rutabaga	Zucchini
Chard	Escarole	Spinach	
Chicory	Green beans	Sprouts	

MILDLY STARCHY VEGETABLES

Artichokes	Carrots	Celery Root	Mushrooms
Beets	Cauliflower	Corn	Peas

IRRITANTS - USE SPARINGLY

Garlic	Leeks	Onions	Radishes

DON'T COMBINE PROTEINS & VEGETABLES WITH FRUITS

☆ EAT FRUIT BY ITSELF ON AN EMPTY STOMACH ☆

LET 1-2 HOURS ELAPSE AFTER EATING FRUIT BEFORE EATING OTHER FOODS

FAIR   FAIR

ACID FRUIT		LOW-ACID FRUIT		SWEET FRUIT	MELON*	
Blackberries	Plums (sour)	Apple	Kiwi	Bananas	Cantaloupe	Honey Dew
Grapefruit	Pomegranate	Apricot	Loquat	Dates	Casaba	Musk
Kumquat	Raspberries	Blueberries	Nectarine	Dried Fruit	Christmas	Persian
Lemon	Strawberries	Cherimoya	Papaya	Grapes	Melon	Sharlyn
Lime	Tangerines	Cherries	Peach	(Thompson	Crenshaw	Watermelon
Orange	Tangelos	Fresh Fig	Pear	& Muscat)		
Pineapple		Grapes	Plums (sweet)	Persimmon		
		Huckleberries		Raisins		

 *Melons are best eaten as a separate meal from other fruits.

Fruits should be eaten as a fruit meal, unmixed with other foods except lettuce and/or celery.

 3-5 hours should elapse after eating other foods before eating fruit again.

 Avocados are best combined with low-starchy vegetables. They make a "fair" combination with starches or acid-fruits.

Tomatoes may be combined with low-starchy vegetables and either nuts or avocados.

Eat only one protein food at a meal.

Fats inhibit the digestion of protein.

Never drink liquids with or immediately following a meal.

FOODS PROPERLY COMBINED *streamline digestion, promote weight loss and energize and strengthen your entire body.*

About Natural Hygiene

The recipes in this book are based on my interpretation of the teachings of natural hygiene. Natural hygiene bases itself upon meeting the needs of humans, strictly in accordance with their biological disposition.

Some important concepts of natural hygiene are:

Health is normal and natural to humans just as with all creatures in nature. Health is produced only by healthful practices.

Disease, sickness, ailments and suffering are abnormal, unnatural and unnecessary, Unhealthful practices inevitably produce disease.

All healing is self-healing. Nothing in the world outside of the body's faculties has the power and intelligence to assess body problems, and to create the cells and fluids necessary to effect tissue repair. "Treatments" from the outside can never substitute for these biological processes and always instead interfere with the them. Diseases do not have to be prevented. They will not happen unless caused.

Health can be regained and maintained only by healthful living. All that is introduced into or onto the body other than those life essentials normal and natural to the body is harmful.

The eating of raw fruits, vegetables, seeds and nuts is but one part of natural hygiene. Natural hygiene is a system of healthful living. To learn more about natural hygiene contact the Natural Hygiene Organizations in the back of this book.

ABOUT THE RECIPES IN THIS BOOK

What Is a Tomatillo?

A tomatillo is a small tomato-like green vegetable with an onion-like skin covering. It is tart. I liquefy it, and use it in place of vinegar. All the major super markets in the West and South West carry tomatillos.

What Is a Jicama?

Although relatively new to North America, the jicama (heecomeah) has flourished in Mexico for centuries. Often called the Mexican potato or yam bean, jicama is the bulbous root of a leguminous plant, resembling a giant brown turnip. It has a thin, patchy, light brown skin, with a crisp, juicy, water chestnut-like interior.

Jicama's white flesh is delightful eaten raw having a distinctive crunchy texture. The flavor is similar to water chestnuts but is sweeter. With only 45 calories for a 3 1/2 ounce serving, jicama is a deliciously dietetic vegetable.

Before serving, peel off skin of desired piece of jicama.

When selecting a jicama choose one that is firm to the touch. Some scarring on the skin is common and does not indicate that the inside flesh is damaged.

Jicama should be stored in a cool dry place. Jicama that has been cut should be sealed with plastic wrap, and refrigerated.

What Is a Daikon?

A daikon is a Japanese white radish that resembles a carrot, but it is usually thicker and longer. I have used this vegetable very sparingly because it mildly contains mustard oil and isothiocyanate, and therefore, irritating to the stomach. It has taken the place of the highly irritating onion which I do not use in my recipes.

What Is Tahini?

Tahini is a thick, smooth paste made of raw, ground sesame seeds.

What Are Bean Sprouts?

Bean sprouts are mung, azuka, and lentil beans that are still in their tiny bean stage, and have not yet fully sprouted. Most health food stores and major grocery chains carry them. If your grocery store does not sell sprouting beans, they can be ordered from

Frieda's of California

P.O. Box 58488

Los Angeles, CA 90008

What Are Tamari, Soy Sauce, & Liquid Aminos?

Tamari is a naturally fermented soy sauce, containing sea salt and alcohol. Some brands contain fermented wheat.

Soy sauce is fermented soy beans, or wheat, or a combination of both. Some brands use yeast and salt. Soy sauce comes in many grades and types, ranging in color from light to dark, in density from thin to thick. Specific types are: light, dark and heavy. Light soy (made with soybean extracts, flour, salt and sugar) is light-colored and delicate. Dark soy (made from the same ingredients, plus caramel) is blacker, richer and thicker. Heavy soy, made with molasses, is thick and sticky.

Liquid Aminos (produced by Bragg), has a soy bean base with a specially formulated vegetable protein.

All three are high in natural sodium. I prefer to use a "mild" style because it has half the sodium content.

How To Wash Spinach

The root must be cut loose from the stems to get all the sand and grit off the small leaves near the root. Rinse spinach in water until all traces of dirt are gone. The leaves will float to the top and the grit will sink. Drain in a colander. Pinch off stems with your fingers, and toss the leaves in cloth towel. If planning to use the spinach soon after washing, spread spinach on another dry towel and place in the refrigerator for at least a half hour to dry the leaves. Dressing will not stick to wet leaves. Otherwise spread the spinach on the towel and roll up the towel. Place in untied plastic bag in the vegetable crisper.

How To Soak Garbanzo Beans (also known as Chick Peas)

Place dry garbanzo beans in a wide-mouth jar or covered casserole dish. Use a proportion of one part beans to three parts water. The beans will triple in size. Always use drinking or distilled water. Put in refrigerator, and shake the jar occasionally. Shaking prevents the beans from pressing against each other when they swell making it difficult to get them out of the jar. Rinse and change the water after the first day. Soak them for two days.

How To Steam Vegetables

For those uninitiated to the eating of raw foods, I have provided some recipes in which the main ingredient is steamed but accompanied by raw food. As your body and attitude becomes acclimated to this change, you will notice that the vegetables taste overcooked, and each time you steam them you will be inclined to lessen the cooking time.

Put 1-1/4 cups to 1-1/2 cups of water into a pot. Don't use tap water. (Fluoride and/or chlorine is put in most drinking water supplies in the country, and they may get into the food.) Insert a steamer. The water level should be below the cage of the steamer to keep nutrients from being lost. Cover the pot, bring the water to a boil, then look into the pot. If you can see the water boiling at the bottom of the steamer, pour a little out. Place vegetables in the steamer. If using an electric stove and the vegetable requires only 4 to 5 minutes cooking time, simply cover the pot, turn off the heat, and keep the pot on the hot grill. It wastes energy to steam food over high heat. The temperature of boiling water and steam remains constant regardless. The coloration that you see in cooking water and the aroma of cooking are evidence of the escape of vitamins and minerals and the destruction of enzymes (valuable amino acids). The latter occurs once food is heated to 120 degrees F. Quick steaming will minimize nutrient losses.

Stoves differ widely. I'm told hy others that the hot plates on my electric stove stay hot longer than theirs. I suggest you experiment with your particular stove. To maintain live steam in the pot, you may have to turn the heat back to medium for a short time after two or three minutes or just leave it on low.

Steaming time also varies with the freshness of the vegetable. For instance, cauliflower and broccoli steam quicker when a week old than when fresh.

How To Clean Vegetables

Wash fruits and vegetables thoroughly before you eat them. I use a product from Amway called LOC, and there are other commercial fruit and vegetable cleaners on the market. Use two tablespoonfuls in a basin or sink of water. Wash fruits and vegetables with a vegetable brush when appropriate. Don't leave fruit in water; wash it quickly to minimize discoloration (oxidizing). Never soak vegetables for more than a few minutes. Rinse thoroughly. Dry with a cloth towel.

I also keep a spray bottle containing a higher concentration of LOC on my sink counter for quick cleaning of single items.

I usually wash all of my fruits and vegetables when I return from the farmer's market. This way there is no confusion as to what is clean and what has to be washed. I make an exception to this rule with asparagus. Otherwise the tips will begin to rot, making the entire stem smell bad in a couple of days. Also, Brussels sprouts should not be washed until just before preparation. I have found that many foods like cucumber, zucchini, spinach, and lettuce stay fresh longer in storage by wrapping them in a dish cloth or towel.

How To Kernel Corn

Place a large bowl in the sink. Twist the corn kerneler over the corn cob while squeezing the kerneler tightly. When you have gone halfway down, flip the cob around, and continue to the end. Go firmly and slowly. Keep the cob pointed well into the bowl because the kerneler will snap when it reaches the end, causing the kernels to scatter. Tap the kerneler clean over the bowl. Using a paring knife and a firm downward motion, scrape the "cream" off the cob into the bowl. Be sure to do this with every cob, because the cream is the tastiest part of the corn. The added flavor is quite noticeable in the recipes.

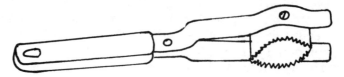

Important Instructions

Many of the foods in this recipe book are to be grated. Although a minimal amount of vitamins and minerals will be lost by grating foods, not only are they easier to eat and digest but they are superior to cooked foods. My hope is to encourage you to eat more raw foods. The Japanese always grate their raw vegetables. Grating releases the flavor and vegetables absorb dressing better. Note: When you have four or five vegetables to grate, refrigerate the cut ones in a covered dish while preparing others. Because vitamin and mineral loss is rapid in cut fruits and vegetables, they should be served immediately.

Seasonings, Condiments & Irritating Foods

You'll notice I use very little seasoning in my recipes. Raw foods don't require seasoning because the natural taste of the food has not been cooked out. All seasonings are optional in the recipes.

Seasoning also increases one's appetite creating an artificial desire for a food that is not physiologically required by the body. Overeating occurs when the appetite is artificially stimulated by seasonings. Without seasonings it is almost impossible to overeat. Seasonings induce eating long after the physiological needs of the body have been fully satisfied.

Also, many seasonings contain salt, garlic, yeast, textured proteins, artificial sweeteners, soybeans, harsh spices and herbs, MSG, fermented residues, and other deleterious substances that should never be taken into our bodies. When buying seasonings always read the label.

Condiments irritate the digestive organs impairing their functioning powers. Salt, spice, vinegar, lemon juice, and all other condiments should not be used.

Such items as onions, garlic, radishes, chili peppers, horseradish, cranberries and all other irritating or bitter foods should be left out of the diet. If they are used at all it should be as sparingly as possible.

Water

While eating, large quantities of digestive juices are being poured into the stomach. If water or beverages are taken, these digestive juices are diluted. The water passes out of the stomach in ten

In addition, drinking water and beverages leads to bolting of food. The food is washed down instead of being properly masticated and salivated. Fermentation, putrefaction, and indigestion will follow. It is recommended that you drink your water:

At least fifteen minutes before meals.

Wait at least thirty minutes after a fruit meal.

Wait at least two hours after a starch meal.

Wait at least four hours after a protein meal.

Desserts

Desserts, eaten at the end of the meal, such as cakes, pies, puddings, ice cream, stewed fruits, etc., do not combine well with vegetable or protein meals, and they cause indigestion. Also, chances are that the eater has already eaten to capacity making it unnecessary to consume more food. Desserts serve no useful purpose and are not advisable. Regarding desserts: DESERT THE DESSERTS.

Raw Food and Saving on Utility Bills

The average family in America can save from $10 to $12 per month on utility bills by switching to a raw food diet. Imagine the reduction of fossil fuel used nationally if this were done!

The cooking of meat and the use of oils in frying creates an estimated 200 pounds of airborne grease per household that is released in the home every year. Some grease may go out the stove exhaust but much is left to coat the walls, cupboards, drapes, floors, windows, window fans and screens, furniture, hair, skin, and nasal passages. Added to this problem is the use of polluting chemicals required to remove the grease. Airborne grease is more carcinogenic than cigarette smoke!

The time saved by not doing the extra cleaning of these items can be better used for productive purposes.

Kitchen Utensils You Will Need

Electric food processor	Chopping board
Manual food grater	Corn kerneler
Electric food blender	Potato peeler
Electric nut chopper/grinder	Julienne cutter (also known as a potato chipper)
Hand-held slicer	An assortment of salad bowls
Assortment of carbon steel knives	

About Aluminum Cookware

Copper and aluminum cookware should not be used if the cooking surface itself is made from either of these metals. Acid foods cooked in aluminum interacts with the metal to form aluminum salts which are toxic. A letter to the New England Journal of Medicine points out the connection between aluminum and brain disorders such as dementia, Alzheimer's disease, behavior abnormalities, poor memory, and impaired visual-motor coordination. One British study shows that aluminum cookware may cause indigestion, heartburn, flatulence, constipation, and headaches. Pots and pans with "no-stick" finishes such as Teflon or Silverstone scratch easily and can contaminate food with bits of plastic while cooking is taking place.

HOW TO SELECT AND STORE FRUIT

The following two chapters have been gleaned from Joe Carcione's The Green Grocer, Jean Anderson Cooks, Don Middaugh, produce marketing manager of Shamrock Foods Co., newspaper food sections, magazine articles, and my own experiences.

In general, never store fruits and vegetables in the same drawer. Fruits produce ethylene gas, which triggers the ripening process. When you combine fruits and vegetables, the gas from the fruit deteriorates the vegetable.

Fruits' ripening time can be determined by controlling the gas. Warm temperatures stimulate ripening; cold temperatures inhibit it. Thus, unripe fruits should ripen at room temperature; ripe fruit should be refrigerated. Remove fruits and tomatoes an hour before serving, as cold temperatures inhibit their flavor.

To speed up ripening, put unripe fruit in a paper bag to concentrate the gas. If the fruit is really hard, add a piece of already ripe fruit. The gas from it will stimulate the gas of the other. An avocado will ripen in three to four days in a paper bag. Add a kiwi or a banana and it will ripen even sooner.

Bananas

It's not true that tree-ripened bananas taste better than artificially ripened ones. If bananas were allowed to ripen before harvesting, they would be starch and mealy or burst out and rotten fruit. Bananas are at their prime when they are a medium yellow color and speckled with brown spots. The speckling indicates they have turned from starch into sugar and are at their sweetest.

Green bananas are placed in air-tight ripening rooms that are scientifically controlled for heat and humidity. This produces a uniformly ripened fruit, with almost all of the starch converted into sugar for good taste.

After a banana ripens it can be refrigerated. To keep it at the peak of ripeness for three days or longer, put it in a dark plastic bag, and seal with a twist tie. The skin may darken but the fruit inside will still be good. Never put a green banana in the refrigerator, If you want to slow down the ripening process, leave them out in the open on a dish in a north-sided room.

Blueberries

Look for plump blueberries. Avoid baskets that are stained with juice. The berries will be soft, watery and overripe.

Shriveled berries indicates they've been held too long since harvesting.

Store blueberries in the container they came in the refrigerator. They will keep a few days, but it's best to use them the same day you buy them. When ready to use, rinse them in cool water.

Cherimoya

Cherimoyas must be handled with care as they are easily damaged and deteriorate rapidly if chilled prior to ripening. They should ripen at room temperature and are best when they are slightly yellow green. Once ripened, cherimoyas can be refrigerated for 3 to 4 days.

Grapefruits and Oranges

As with all citrus, the heavier the fruit, the juicier. Florida grapefruits and oranges are juicer than those from California and Arizona, but Western fruit has a thicker skin that's easier to peel. Unchilled oranges lose juice. Refrigerated oranges and grapefruits both keep for a few weeks.

Grapes

Grapes should be plump and firm. Purple varieties should be a robust, deep color. Green seedless varieties should be yellowish in color. When they are more green than yellow they are not fully ripe. Bunches with small green berries indicate underdevelopment, and will be sour. A good indication is the velvety powdery look on the skin.

Grapes should be kept refrigerated to prevent dehydration. Pick off any bad grapes before you put them in a plastic bag. They will keep up to two weeks. Rinse grapes when you're ready to serve them.

Kiwis

To select a ripe Kiwi, place one in the palm of your hand and squeeze very gently. As you add pressure the fruit should give slightly. If you prefer to ripen it at home, place it in the same bag as your bananas. The fruit will ripen uniformly.

Ripe kiwis will stay fresh in the refrigerator for several weeks.

Mango

Select a smooth-skinned mango that has started to gain color. All-green ones may never ripen properly. Avoid shriveled fruit and those with large black areas on the skin. They are overripe.

To ripen a mango place in a paper bag on top of the refrigerator where the temperature is warm and constant. A mango is ready to eat when it yields to pressure when cradled in the palm. A truly ripe mango will also produce a rich aromatic, fruity scent. Once it's ripe, refrigerate in a plastic bag.

Sweet Melons

Varieties of this fruit include cantaloupe, Persian melons, Crenshaw melons, casaba melons, and honey dew melons. A general comment about selection is don't select soft melons; they will always be overripe. Any mellon that "sloshes" when shaken will be mushy inside and may have started to sour. Reject any melons that are soft and wet at the stem end, they have already started to decay and will deteriorate rapidly. Melons become riper and mellower after they are picked, but their sugar content does not increase. Keep melons in a warm area out of direct sunlight for three or four days before chilling and serving. Store cut melons in the refrigerator with the seeds in, wrapped in plastic. Eat within a few days.

Individual Melon Information

A ripe cantaloupe will be completely covered with a creamy-colored netting against a creamy yellow background. The smell will be sweet and musky and the blossom end (opposite the stem end) will yield slightly when pressed. Don't select one that has a large smooth spot on the surface.

Persian melons resemble oversized cantaloupes, but are rounder with a finer, flatter netting. Select a springy melon devoid of large smooth spots. Avoid those with a dark or greenish-black netting; a sign of immaturity which probably won't ripen successfully.

Casaba melons: Choose a golden-yellow one which will spring back when the blossom end is gently pressed.

Honey dew melons should be selected by having a creamy-white or creamy-yellow color rind. The skin should have a soft velvety feel, slightly sticky or oily.

Nectarines

Select nectarines that are firm, plump and well-formed. Skin color should show a blush of bright red over a yellow or yellow-orange background. Avoid green or dull-colored fruit. It was picked too early and will shrivel instead of ripening.

If you wish to store the fruit before ripening, they will keep well in the refrigerator.

Oranges

Not all oranges are orange-colored; many are green. The cool climate in California and Arizona is what makes oranges turn orange-colored. Because of customer preference, oranges from Florida and Texas are put in a dye-bath that changes their color from their natural green to orange. They are always stamped "Color Added." In California, Valencia oranges tend to regreen late in the season. Don't judge an orange by its color. Select ones that are firm and heavy for their size; an indication of a juicy orange. Choose smooth-skinned ones.

Store oranges in a cool place. The refrigerator is acceptable but not necessary. If a mold develops on an orange, get rid of it before it spreads to other fruit.

Papayas

Papayas ripen from the blossom-end up to the stem-end. A good papaya has started to color and has speckled yellow over 35% of the fruit. At that point, the fruit will ripen completely in two to three days at room temperature.

Select one with a fruity aroma which yields under slight pressure. The skin should be smooth, not shrivelled. Dark skinned ones with dark spots will get progressively worse and eventually penetrate through the flesh and cause a bad flavor.22

A ripe papaya can be stored in the refrigerator for one or two days.

Peaches

A pink or red color on a peach may look attractive but it is not a good indication of ripeness and flavor. A better tasting fruit has a yellowish or creamy background color. Judge by aroma. The best peaches will have a good peachy fragrance.

Don't buy a peach that is green around the stem; it was picked too soon and didn't have a chance to develop its sugar content. The peach will soften but not ripen, giving it that mushy consistency.

To ripen a peach fully, put it in a brown paper bag, seal it and leave it on the counter. It should ripen within two days. Soft fruit should be eaten within a day or two as peaches rot rapidly.

Store peaches unwashed in the refrigerator. They should keep for two weeks.

Pears

Unripe pears are tasteless. Pears are picked unripe and must be ripened at home. Select pears that are free from cuts or dark spots.

The best place to ripen pears is on top of the refrigerator where the temperature is warm and even. When placed in a plastic bag, poke holes in the bag. They will ripen in two or three days. The pear is ready to eat when it is gently pressed against the side and there is a little give. After pears ripen they should be refrigerated,

Persimmons

Persimmon is one fruit that is not selected by appearance. Persimmons are unique – they get their full color before they're ripe. If you eat a persimmon that is not ripe, you probably will never want to eat one again, so be sure it's ripe.

The persimmon must be very soft, even shriveled. The fruit should be plump, with smooth shiny skin and the green stem attached.

Persimmons ripen evenly when placed in the same paper sack as your ripening bananas.

Pineapples

A good pineapple has a yellow to golden orange glow under the skin, a fresh green crown, and a good scent. Avoid pineapples with bruises, discolored areas, soft spots or dried-out brownish leaves, a shriveled appearance or dull color. A pineapple does not ripen once picked, so assuming you have a ripe one, eat it within a day or two.

Store pineapples by placing them in a plastic bag to prevent moisture loss, and they should keep three to five days in the refrigerator.

Plums

Choose plums that have good color for their variety, and yield to gentle pressure. They should be slightly soft at the tip. If they are not quite ripe yet, let them ripen a day or two at room temperature in a paper bag. Then store them in the refrigerator, uncovered for up to 5 days.

Pomegranates

Select fruit with good color and skin that's free from cracks or splits.

Store in a plastic bag in the refrigerator. They will keep several weeks.

Strawberries

Select plump heart-shaped berries with a natural shine, rich, red color and fresh-looking green caps.

Strawberries do not ripen after picking, so they can be stored in the refrigerator until ready to eat. To maintain flavor, appearance and nutrition, store strawberries in their basket, not an airtight container, and cover loosely with a plastic wrap. Check the basket and throw out any bad strawberries. Allow strawberries to reach room temperature before serving.

Just before using, rinse strawberries with caps still attached under a gentle spray of cool water; pat dry with a cloth napkin. (I don't put paper towels in contact with food because the towels are coated with formaldehyde). Do not remove the green caps before washing. The caps prevent water from breaking down the flavor and the texture inside the berries.

When caps should be removed, give them a slight twist, or use the point of a sharp paring knife.

Tangerines & Tangelos

Select ones with a deep rich color having a bright luster. The fruit should feel heavy for its size. A slightly puffy appearance is normal because of the loose skin. Excessive puffiness may indicate overripe fruit. Avoid skin with very soft spots or mold.

Tangerines and tangelos don't keep as well as sweet oranges. Store them in the fruit bin in the refrigerator.

Watermelon

produce managers claim that thumping, slapping and shaking is not a good test for selecting a good watermelon. There is no sure way of picking a good one but there are a few ways to avoid picking a "lemon." It should have a velvety bloom on the rind. Avoid ones with a shiny appearance. The "belly" of the watermelon is where it rested on the ground. The color should be slightly yellowish or amber-colored. Avoid any with a greenish or dead-white color in that area.

When buying a cut watermelon, look for firm red flesh and black or dark-brown seeds. Avoid watermelon with soft, white immature seeds, or ones that have broken away from their cavities, or ones with a sugary look around the seeds. And lastly, reject watermelon with a white streak running the length of the melon.

Watermelons can be stored for up to a week in the refrigerator.

HOW TO SELECT AND STORE VEGETABLES

Asparagus

Fresh asparagus has tips that are well-formed, tightly closed, and come to a point. If the tips are open or have gone to seed the asparagus may be usable but is past its prime. If the tips are wet or slimy, this is a sign of decay. Bright-green spears with white ends retain moisture better than all-green spears. As in most cases your nose should be able to pick out a fresh bunch. Look for firm straight stalks with green stems about two-thirds of their length. Limp, wilted stalks and ones that are flat or angular will probably be tough and stringy.

Use asparagus as soon as possible. If you are not going to use asparagus within two days, cut 1/2 off the bottoms, wrap the butt ends with a damp cloth in a plastic bag. Place in the vegetable crisper.

When preparing, snap off the tough woody part of each stalk at the point where it will break easily (where the green and white blend).

Avocados

A mature avocado has a full neck. It is better to buy an unripe avocado and ripen it at home, because ripe ones tend to be bruised from handling. An avocado is ripe when it yields to gentle pressure when cradled in the palm. The hard, bumpy skinned varieties will ripen very easily. The smooth skinned varieties will ripen if they haven't been picked too green.

The fastest way to ripen an avocado is to wrap it in foil so the natural ripening gases can be contained. I save packaged foil bags and fold the bag around one or two avocados sealing it with a loose rubber band. A bit slower process is to place the avocado in a paper bag, and placing it on top of the refrigerator where the temperature is warm and even.

After the avocado is ripened, it will keep, uncut, in the refrigerator for four to seven days. Place it on a flat surface or in a bowl. The shelf grates will cause indentations on ripened avocados. Never place an unripened avocado in the refrigerator.

Beets

For tenderness, select small, smooth, unbroken skins around the crown, and a round rather than an oblong shape. Large beets are apt to be tough and have a woody texture. The root should be smooth and firm. The tops, if any, should have crinkly, dark green leaves.

Bell Peppers

Bell peppers should be firm, smooth, thick flesh, without soft or brown spots and have a shiny, strong color (red or green). Check the stem end, which withers first. The red bell pepper is simply the green pepper that has matured on the vine. It contains more vitamin C and is sweeter to the taste.

Bell peppers tend to get soft on the ends, shrivel and mold when exposed to humidity. Store them in airtight containers or in the refrigerator drawer. Some grown peppers should be lightly oiled with vegetable oil.

Broccoli

The stalks should be tender and firm. The heads should be compact and dark green or purplish-green. Overmaturity is indicated by flowering yellow buds. Broccoli should smell fresh.

Store by removing any wilted leaves and slice off the coarse stem ends. Wrap the base of each stem in a damp – not wet – cloth. I don't use paper towels, because they are treated with formaldehyde. Place broccoli in a plastic bag but don't seal. Refrigerate. Broccoli does not retain its nutrients very well after harvesting. Use it as soon as possible.

Brussels Sprouts

Select uniformly small, firm, compact heads with bright green color. Wilted yellow leaves are a sign of age meaning they will be tough and strong-flavored. Also to be avoided, are large puffy ones or heads with black spots or holes which show insect damage.

Brussels sprouts are highly perishable. Keep refrigerated. Don't wash until just prior to use. Use within a day or two.

Cabbage

Look for smooth, unblemished, crisp, compact heads of bright color that feel heavy for their size. Exception: Savoy is more loose than other cabbages, but its inner leaves should be tightly headed. Cabbage becomes dehydrated when the butt ends have been excessively trimmed. Very large, hard heads may be overmature and taste strong or bitter.

Most varieties of cabbage can be stored for at least a week. Rinse in cool water, place in an untied plastic bag and store in the vegetable crisper. I gently peel away the outer leaves, keeping them attached at the butt, then fold them over the cut end when storing unused portions.

Carrots

Look for crispness and moistness, uniformity of size, well-shaped and medium dark color. Small carrots are more tasty. Avoid limp, rubbery ones with nicks, bumps, blemishes, cracks or splits. The best carrots are those with the tops on them. If they are crisp and frilly, you can be sure they are fresh,

The tops drain moisture from the carrot, so they should be removed 1" above the crown before refrigerating. Rinse in cool water. Place in an untied plastic bag and put in vegetable crisper.

Cauliflower

Look for compact white or ivory heads, tightly curded, with crinkly green jacket leaves at the base. Avoid bruised, blemished or loose and spread out heads, which are a sure sign of overmaturity, wrap loosely in a plastic bag.

Celery

Stalks should be ultracrisp not limp and pliable. Avoid ones with cracks or blemishes and crinkly yellow-green leaves.

Before storing, remove any coarse outer ribs that may be bruised, and after cutting away any discolored, cracked or soft portions, package them separately. Always cut away the brown portion on the bottom. The change in color show decay. Cut 1/8 inch off end and top, and immerse celery in 100 degree water for 15 minutes. Drain for 10 minutes and put in an airtight crisper. Celery will stay crisp for four weeks.

Corn

The sugar in the kernels start to convert into starch the moment corn is harvested. Use as soon as possible. Select corn that is tightly sheathed in crisp green husks with silvery-gold tassels. Withered brown or dry tassels indicate that the corn has not been harvested recently. Pull the husk away a few inches and select ones where the kernels are plump, milky and tender, and come all the way to the ear's tip. They should be large enough so there's no space between the rows. Kernels that are dented indicate age.

Cucumbers

Select straight, uniformly firm cucumbers devoid of nicks and blemishes. Avoid ones that are puffy in appearance with a dull color, sometimes yellowed. Wrinkly, shriveled cucumbers will have a tough and bitter tasting skin. Dark and sunken areas indicate decay. Small ones are usually best.

Cucumbers get soft on the ends, shrivel and mold if there's any humidity. Store them in airtight containers or in the refrigerator drawer at a temperature no less than 45 degrees. Wrap in a cloth napkin to absorb excess moisture which helps slow the softening process. Cucumbers from home gardens should be slightly oiled with vegetable oil before refrigerating.

Cucumbers are often waxed so they'll hold their moisture longer. Try to avoid them because unwaxed cucumbers can be eaten peel and all and are much more nutritious.

Eggplant

Tales to the contrary, there is no way to distinguish "male" from "female" eggplants and thus, presumably, to know which ones harbor fewer seeds.

Good eggplant is firm and has a bright, shiny, dark color. Gently heft the eggplant to determine if it's heavy for it's size, the way it should be. Avoid one's that feel flabby or shriveled. Large eggplants and those with soft, brown patches may be bitter. Eggplant bruises easily, so watch for signs of scarring that show up as dark spots on the surface.

Keep eggplant refrigerated or it will start losing moisture and become soft and shriveled. Eggplant is fragile so don't pile other produce on top of it. Don't put eggplant in a plastic bag. Store in the vegetable crisper.

Fennel or Finocchino

Fennel is related to the celery family. It has frilly leaves, round stalks and a large bulbous root with the sweet aroma of anise or licorice.

Fresh bulbs are compact, moist and crisp. Avoid ones that have cuts on the surface, yellowed or are overly coarse. Flowers in the central seed stems are a sign of overmaturity.

Store fennel in a plastic bag in the refrigerator for a few days before using. When using in salads, slice thinly starting from the bottom. Do not discard the feathery top, which is very tasty. The toughest portions of the hollow stems may have to be discarded, but the tender stems can be used.

Okra

Also known as Chinese okra and pleated squash. They are long, narrow, and light-green. Okra's are segmented lengthwise, with sharp, tough edges. They have a refreshing, slightly sweet taste. Wash and store in vegetable bin.

To use, cut away hard stringy edges. Scrape skin.

Parsnips

Look for small to medium, smooth, well-shaped parsnips. Large parsnips tend to have woody cores. A soft parsnip indicates age and will be fibrous and pithy.

To store cut off tops (they will sap the parsnip), then bag loosely in plastic in the refrigerator.

Peas (green)

Pods should be firm, bright green, and crisp, and squeak when rubbed together. Peas begin to lose their sugar immediately on picking, so use as soon as possible.

Store in pods up to two days in coldest part of refrigerator.

Spinach

Spinach should have bright-green color and tender leaves.

Wash well. Drain and store in crisper or in a plastic Sag up to five days.

Sweet Potatoes and Yams

The best quality are small- or medium-sized that taper at both ends. They should be firm, well-shaped with a smooth skin. Avoid ones with growth cracks, discolored, or surface injury. Yams should be moist with bright orange color. Sweet potatoes should be dry, and a light yellow to tan color.

Store sweet potatoes and yams in a basket in a dry, cool, well-ventilated place. Do not refrigerate. They will keep for two to four weeks.

Squash (Zucchini, Yellow, Acorn, Summer, Banana)

In general, all squash should have good color, firm body, and smooth rind.

Soft-shell "summer" squashes – such as zucchini and yellow squash – are harvested young, have edible thin skins and soft seeds. The tastiest are small; the freshest are firm with smooth, shiny skin. Refrigerate in plastic bag up to one week.

Hard-shell "winter" squashes – like acorn, butternut and pumpkin – mature on the vine. Skins and seeds are tough. Buy them hard and heavy for their size, with a dull finish, Store "winter" squashes in dry, cool place.

Tomatoes

Tomatoes sold in supermarkets are usually picked green and are tasteless. Cherry and Italian plum tomatoes are slightly better than the beefsteak variety. Pink-orange tomatoes redden in four days. Fully ripe tomatoes are deep reddish-orange. Select tomatoes by their aroma. They should smell deliciously of tomato flavor. They should yield to slight pressure. A locally grown, blemished tomato is better than a perfect "plastic" one. Other qualities to look for are red, firm, well-shaped tomatoes.

Store ripe tomatoes by spreading out on a cool, dark dry shelf for a day or two. Don't stack tomatoes in a bowl or they will soften on the spots that touch each other. Make "pockets" by using a dish towel to prevent the tomatoes from touching each other. Ripen green tomatoes by placing them in a perforated bag with an apple. Keep out of direct sunlight. They will ripen suddenly, so check every day. Never refrigerate unripe tomatoes. Cold temperatures trap the gas in them, causing them to turn mushy. When tomatoes become overripe, the loss of vitamin C is increased. If you must refrigerate ripe tomatoes, do so only briefly.

Turnips and Rutabagas

Small turnips and rutabagas are sweeter and more tender. Large ones may be woody or pithy. Look for roots that are heavy for their size. Avoid any with cuts from mechanical harvesting.

My resources differ on whether turnips and rutabagas should be refrigerated. Refrigerated ones, kept in a plastic bag will keep for up to one month. When kept in a cool humid place they will keep for two to three weeks. Turnip greens, however, are perishable and should be refrigerated and used within a few days.

But once we become aware of the impact of our food choices, we can never really forget. For the earth itself will remind us, as will our children and the animals and the forests and the sky and the rivers - that we are part of this earth, and it is part of us. All things are deeply connected, and so the choices we make in our daily lives have enormous influence, not only on our own health and vitality - but also on the lives of other beings, and indeed on the destiny of life on earth. John Robbins 1988.

Hors D'Oeuvres

We spend the first half of our lives wasting our health to gain wealth. And the second half of our lives spending our wealth to regain our health. Author Unknown

The healthier you are, the easier it will be to control your thinking and recondition yourself to a sane way of living. The more physically healthy you become, the less effort it takes to control your emotions. The reverse is also true; the more control you have over your emotions, the more physically healthy you will become. It works both ways. Dr. Virginia Vetrano, 1988.

If you don't find time for exercise now, you will have to find time for illness later! Wayne Pickering, 1982.

FRUIT KEBABS

APPLE TWIST KEBAB

Pour 2 cups of ORGANIC APPLE JUICE with 1 tablespoon LIME or LEMON JUICE in a small bowl. Put all fruit into bowl as you cut them. Peel a RED APPLE in one continuous peel. Cut APPLE, PEAR, PLUM, and FRESH FIG into chunks. Push only one end of apple peel on skewer. Let hang. Slide fruit chunks on skewer. Twist apple peel around chunks of fruit. Push chunks to the end of skewer to get end of apple peel on. Slide back into center. Pour apple juice over top. Sprinkle with ALLSPICE

CITRUS/ACID KEBAB

Chunks of PINEAPPLE, ORANGE slices, STRAWBERRIES, with chunks of center section of FENNEL in between each fruit. Liquify strawberries in nut chopper, and pour over top. Season with ALLSPICE. (All spices are optional).

LOW-ACID FRUIT KEBAB

APRICOT chunks, MANGO chunks, CHERRIES. Liquefy cherries in nut chopper, and pour over top. Season with CINNAMON.

SWEET FRUIT KEBAB

Sliced BANANA, DATES, PERSIMMON. Liquify with equal amounts of sweet grapes and pre-soaked raisins in nut chopper. Pour over top. Season with ANISE.

TART TREAT KEBAB

Chunks of PINEAPPLE, KIWI, and STRAWBERRY, with BLACKBERRIES between each fruit. Liquefy plums or grapes, and pour over top.

GREEN CREPES

Use soft lettuce leaves like Boston Lettuce or Red Leaf Lettuce to roll up any of the combinations below:

Soften AVOCADO with LEMON JUICE and add fresh CORN, diced BANANA PEPPER and chopped PIMIENTOS. Season with KELP.

1 cup finely grated CARROTS, 1/8 cup SUNFLOWER SEEDS, 3 tablespoons finely chopped CELERY. Season lightly with DILL.

Dice a CUCUMBER. Add fresh YOUNG PEAS, and finely diced TOMATOES and GREEN PEPPER. Season with fresh, minced BASIL.

1 cup BEAN SPROUTS, 1/8 cup raw, chopped PEPITAS. 1/4 cup diced CUCUMBER, 1/8 cup chopped PARSLEY, 1 tablespoon minced DAIKON.

One ZUCCHINI and CARROT, finely shredded. 2 tablespoons chopped DAIKON. Season with fresh, minced SWEET BASIL.

One cup coarsely grated JICAMA. 1/4 cup diced CELERY or FENNEL. 1/2 cup chopped ALFALFA SPROUTS, 1/4 cup chopped WATERCRESS, 2 tablespoons finely grated DAIKON.

One cup finely grated PARSNIPS. 1/2 cup grated CARROTS. 1/4 cup chopped FENNEL. 3 tablespoons chopped SUNFLOWER SEEDS. 1/2 teaspoon ground NUTMEG (optional).

Put spoonfuls of the mixture onto the lettuce leaves. Carefully roll up, and spear with a cocktail stick. Garnish with a BLACK or STUFFED GREEN OLIVE.

SALAD KEBABS

Combine any of the following group on a skewer.

CAULIFLOWER florets, CHERRY TOMATOES, chopped sweet green PEPPER, stuffed GREEN OLIVE.

BROCCOLI, MUSHROOMS, ZUCCHINI chunks, BLACK OLIVES

ZUCCHINI slices, SNOWPEAS cut in 1" lengths, BANANA PEPPER, all intertwined with strips of PIMIENTOS.

Place skewers on a bed of sliced lettuce with dressing of your choice.

SPROUTED GARBANZO CROQUETTES

1 cup sprouted GARBANZO BEANS, ground with food processor

1/4 cup finely chopped, PARSLEY

1/2 cup CARROT JUICE with pulp

1/4 cup minced DAIKON

1 tablespoon powdered BOUILLON

1/2 cup raw SESAME SEEDS

Combine all ingredients except seeds. Form into balls. Roll in seeds and serve on a bed of lettuce. Serves two.

STUFFED FENNEL

Use the centers of the FENNEL, and slice lengthwise if necessary. Put a heaping tablespoon of ALMOND BUTTER in nut chopper, add enough distilled water to soften. Remove from chopper and add diced CUCUMBER and grated CARROT. Sprinkle with chopped ALFALFA SPROUTS.

STUFFED PEPPER STRIPS

Cut into quarters 1 each RED, YELLOW and GREEN BELL PEPPERS. Put 1 cup sprouted SUNFLOWER SEEDS in nut chopper and chop slightly. In a separate bowl, add 1/2 cup finely grated CARROTS, 1 small AVOCADO, diced, 1/2 cup chopped ALFALFA SPROUTS, and 1/2 cup finely diced CUCUMBER. Mix well. Spoon onto peppers. Mix the colors when placing on serving dish.

Fruit Drinks

Men dig their Graves with their own Teeth and die more by those fated Instruments than by the Weapons of their Enemies. Thomas Moffett, 1600.

What is impossible to see from the viewpoint of those who believe in "cures" is that the very symptoms the good doctors have suppressed and turned into chronic disease were the body's only means of correcting the problem! The so-called "disease" was the only "cure" possible. Dr. Phillip Chapman, 1981.

You have a new body every seven years! Virtually all tissue has been replaced within that period of time. Dr. Keki Sidhwa, 1969.

APPLE SAPOTE CHERRY DRINK

2 cups organic APPLE juice

1 cup chopped SAPOTE

1/2 cup CHERRIES

Combine all ingredients in electric blender. Serves two.

BANANA SHAKE

1 small PAPAYA, peeled, pitted, chopped

2 ripe BANANAS, quartered

2 tablespoons ALMOND BUTTER (any nut butter except peanut).

Put papaya in blender and puree. Put in banana and blend for three seconds. Put in almond butter. Blend for five seconds. To eat, pour in a dish. Serve immediately. Serves two.

BLUEBERRY APPLE DRINK

2 cups organic APPLE juice

1 cup BLUEBERRIES

1 cup white, seedless GRAPES

1 tablespoon LEMON juice

Blend all ingredients in electric blender. Serves 2.

CHERRY APPLE DRINK

1 cup FRESH CHERRIES, pitted

2 APPLES, chopped

Put cherries and apples in blender and liquefy. Serve immediately. Serves two.

GRAPE APRICOT DRINK

2 cups organic GRAPE juice

1 cup chopped ripe APRICOTS

1 stalk chopped CELERY

Blend all ingredients in electric blender. Serves two.

ORANGE LOGANBERRY DRINK

2 cups ORANGE juice

1 cup LOGANBERRIES

1 chopped CELERY stalk

Blend all ingredients in electric blender. Serves two.

PEACH, PEAR & PLUM DRINK

2 large PEACHES, quartered

2 large PLUMS, quartered

2 PEARS, quartered

1/2 cup BLACKBERRIES, mashed with fork

Combine peaches, plums and pears in blender and liquefy. Pour into chilled juice glasses. Spoon blackberries over top.

PERSIMMON SHAKE

2 ripe PERSIMMONS, quartered

4 pre-soaked dried FIGS, quartered

2 pre-soaked dried APRICOTS, quartered

2 tablespoons ALMOND or PECAN BUTTER

Put all in blender and puree. Serve immediately. Serves two.

PINEAPPLE DRINK

3 cups PINEAPPLE chunks

1 CELERY* rib with leaves, chopped

1 PEAR, quartered

1 cup white seedless grapes

Combine all ingredients in blender and liquefy. Chill. Serve immediately. Serves two.

*Celery is an alkaline vegetable. It neutralizes the acid in the pineapple.

Nut & Seed Milks

Think of the fierce energy concentration in an acorn! You bury it in the ground, and it explodes into a great oak! Bury a sheep and nothing happens but decay. George Bernard Shaw

It's great to let food be a pleasure! Just don't let food be your only treasure! Victoria Bid Well

Forbear, mortals, to pollute your bodies with the flesh of animals. There is corn; there are the apples that bear down the branches by their weight; and there are the grapes, nuts, and vegetables. These shall be our food. Pythagoras, 582 B.C.

ALMOND MILK

3/4 cup ALMONDS, CASHEWS, SESAME SEEDS, SUNFLOWER SEEDS,
  or any combination

2 cups COLD DRINKING WATER

1 DATE, skinned, peeled

When using almonds it's best to soak them overnight then remove the bitter skins by blanching. Grind nuts in blender. Add 1 cup water and date. Blend on high for one minute. Slowly add remaining water. Blend for one minute. Pour through fine strainer. Serves two. Serve immediately.

SWEET SEED MILK

3/4 cup SUNFLOWER SEEDS

1/4 cup SESAME SEEDS

4 cups COLD DRINKING WATER

10 DATES, remove pits and hard stalks

Grind the seeds out finely in blender. Add two cups of water and blend on high for one minute. Add the dates and blend for half minute. Add remaining water and blend for one minute. Serves two. Serve immediately.

Variation: Add one banana and 1/2 cup of water.

Fruit Dishes

The Standard American Diet is a pathogenic arrangement that is responsible for a long list of diseases. This is evident when a mere change in diet enables SAD Sufferers to become free of their problems and lead healthful lives! T.C. Fry 1989.

A short life is not given us, but we ourselves make it so. Seneca, 62 A.D.

One organ will not be diseased all by itself and the rest of the body remain healthy. Treating affected organs or tissues as entities is short-sighted and not based on sound science. There is unity of the body, as there is unity of the Universe. Remove all disease by removing or correcting the primary causes. Specialization in medicine is, therefore, nothing but a form of tinkering or patchwork. Dr. Virginia Ventrano, 1968

APPLE BLUEBERRY PUDDING*

2 sweet APPLES, chopped. Sprinkle with lemon or lime.

1 basket BLUEBERRIES

3/4 cup BARLEY

1 cup organic APPLE JUICE

1/2 cup chopped ALMONDS

dash of CINNAMON

Soak barley in apple juice overnight.

Drain excess juice from barley if desired. Combine ingredients except cinnamon. Scoop in desert dish. Sprinkle with cinnamon, Serves two.

*This dish requires overnight soaking.

BANANA BLUEBERRY PIE

Basket of BLUEBERRIES

2 medium BANANAS

PIE CRUST

2/3 cup pre-soaked SUNFLOWER SEEDS

2/3 cup pre-soaked ALMONDS

2/3 cup pre-soaked RAISINS

1/2 cup COCONUT

1/4 cup ALMOND OIL

Pie crust: Soak first three ingredients overnight. Drain. Grind all ingredients in a food processor. Place in a twelve-inch pie dish and pat in place with a tablespoon. Chill and fill with sliced bananas and blueberries. Can mix bananas and blueberries together before putting in pie crust, or place bananas around edge with blueberries in center. Serves four.

BANANA DELIGHT

6 pre-soaked DRIED FIGS

1/8 cup pre-soaked RAISINS

1/2 cup sweet GRAPES

2 BANANAS, sliced in half lengthwise

1 SAPOTE, sliced (optional)

6 RED CHERRIES

Place figs, raisins, and grapes in a blender using just enough of the soaking water to puree. Pour over banana and sapote. Top with cherries. Serves two.

BANANA "ICE CREAM"

(Must have a Champion Juicer to make this. Worth buying a Champion Juicer for!)

2 or 3 bananas per serving

1/3 cup raisins per serving

Peel ripe (speckled on skin) bananas. Wrap plastic wrap around each banana to keep air tight. Or you can roll them in a plastic bag keeping them separate. Store in freezer for 10 hours or more. Freeze raisins.

Bananas can be used alone or try freezing other fruits like, blackberries, pineapple, figs, pitted dates, peaches, or persimmons.

Almonds can be soaked overnight (just enough distilled water to cover them). Pour off water and freeze. Add while bananas are being processed.

Complete directions for making banana "ice cream" are in the Champion Juicer instruction booklet.

BLUEBERRY, LOQUAT & BANANA DISH

1 cup BLUEBERRIES

4 LOQUATS

2 small, ripe BANANAS, sliced thin

1/2 cup pre-soaked, chopped FIGS or DATES, pitted and chopped

1/2 cup GRAPES

Blend half the blueberries in an electric blender. Add grapes.

Blend for a few seconds. Turn blender to low speed and add figs or dates gradually. Don't use figs and dates in the same recipe. Put loquats and banana and remaining blueberries in dessert dish. Pour fruit syrup over top. Serves two.

BLUEBERRY PIE*

1 basket BLUEBERRIES

1/2 cup chopped, pre-soaked dried APPLES

1/2 teaspoon ground CINNAMON

Crust:

2/3 cup SUNFLOWER SEEDS

2/3 cup ALMONDS

2/3 cup RAISINS

2/3 cup shredded COCONUT

1/4 cup ALMOND OIL

Crust: Soak first three ingredients overnight in distilled water. Also at this time, soak the apples and cinnamon using distilled water. Drain and rinse sunflower and almonds. Grind all ingredients in a food processor. Pat into individual desert dishes. Chill for half hour. Fill with blueberry. Sprinkle with apples. Serves four.

*This dish requires overnight soaking.

BREAKFAST PARFAIT

In stemmed glasses, layer sliced strawberries, kiwi, blackberries or blueberries. Repeat layers, ending with strawberries with either a slice of kiwi in center or three blackberries.

CHERIMOYA
(also called Custard Apple)

2 Cherimoyas

2 Kiwis

1 cup seedless Grapes (any variety)

shredded COCONUT (optional)

Cut cherimoya in quarters. Remove as many seeds as possible.

Remove from skin in bite-size pieces with a spoon. Peel, quarter and slice kiwi. Mix fruits together. Chill slightly if desired. Sprinkle with coconut. Serves two.

CITRUS FRUIT DELIGHT

1 PINK GRAPEFRUIT, cut in half, remove sections

1 large ORANGE, peeled, pull sections off, cut in half

1 KIWI, peeled, quartered lengthwise, sliced

1/2 cup diced tender center of CELERY

Combine fruit. Sprinkle with celery. Can top with BLACKBERRIES or STRAWBERRIES. Chill or serve immediately. Serves two.

COLD FRUIT COMPOTE*

1/2 cup dried APRICOTS

3/4 cup dried APPLES

1/2 cup dried FIGS

2 slices dried PINEAPPLE

1 1/2 cups APPLE or GRAPE JUICE

Chop fruit in 1/2 inch pieces and soak overnight in juice. Keep refrigerated. Serve the next day. Serve in chilled, stemmed glasses. Serves two.

*This dish requires overnight soaking.

EXOTIC FRUIT MEDLEY

2 SAPOTES, peeled, pitted, chopped

1 small CHERIMOYA, peeled, pitted, chopped

1 PERSIMMON, chopped

1/2 cup fresh BLUEBERRIES

4 presoaked DRIED FIGS, chopped

1/2 cup DISTILLED WATER

Pre-soak figs overnight with distilled water. Combine first three ingredients. Sprinkle with blueberries and figs. Pour soaking water from figs over top. Chill or serve immediately. Serves two.

FEYOA FRUIT BOWL

3 FEYOAS (also called pineapple guava) peeled, cubed

1/2 cup ripe GOOSEBERRIES

1 PEAR, cubed

1 KIWI, peeled, cubed

3/4 cup organic APPLE juice

Combine fruit and pour juice over top. Serves two.

FRESH & DRIED FRUIT DISH

6 FIGS (pre-soaked overnight with just enough distilled water to cover)

2 PEACHES, sliced

2 APRICOTS, sliced

1/3 cup RAISINS (pre-soaked)

1/2 cup GRAPES

1/3 cup CHERRIES

Chop figs. Combine first three ingredients. Put raisins and grapes in blender (nut chopper is effective for small amounts). Use just enough soaking water to puree. Swirl until smooth. Pour over fruit. Garnish with cherries. Serves two.

FRUIT DISH with DRIED APRICOT TOPPING

2 ripe PEACHES, peel off skin, cut into chunks

2 ripe PLUMS, peel off skin, cut into chunks

4 presoaked FIGS, remove stem, quartered

6 dried pre-soaked APRICOTS

1/4 teaspoon ground CINNAMON

1/2 cup GRAPES

1/3 cup pre-soaked RAISINS (optional)

Pre-soak apricots and cinnamon overnight with just enough water to cover. Combine first three ingredients. put apricots and grapes in nut chopper or blender with just enough soaking water to puree. Pure over fruit. Top with raisins. Serve immediately. Serves two.

MORNING FRUIT DISH

3 or 4 BANANAS

1 PAPAYA

3/4 to 1 cup PAPAYA or MANGO PUREE

(found in health food stores, or you can make your own in a blender)

1/2 cup pre-soaked RAISINS

Slice bananas thin (they seem sweeter that way). Scoop papaya from skin and cut in chunks. Mix together. Pour puree over fruit. Sprinkle with raisins. Serves two.

PEAR APPLE FRUIT DISH

2 PEARS

2 APPLES

1 cup ALFALFA SPROUTS

1/2 cup pre-soaked RAISINS or can use grapes or cherries

1 cup unfiltered APPLE JUICE

Cut pears and apples into mouth size pieces. Remove seeds. Sprinkle alfalfa sprouts on top. Garnish with raisins or grapes or cherries. Pour juice over top. Serves two.

PEAR & CHERRY with PLUM SYRUP

2 PEARS

1 cup fresh CHERRIES, pitted

2 PLUMS

1/2 cup pre-soaked RAISINS

Cut pears into bite-size pieces. Mix with cherries in desert dish. Put plums and raisins in blender with just enough of the soaking water to blend. Pour over top. Serves two.

PINEAPPLE ICE DESERT

1 small can un-sweetened, frozen, concentrated PINEAPPLE juice

1 PAPAYA, cut in half, seeded, removed from skin, chopped

2 NECTARINES, chopped

1/2 cup CURRANTS

Remove pineapple juice from freezer one hour before preparing. Don't dilute it. Put all ingredients in electric blender. Liquefy. Freeze to a semi-solid state. Serves four.

PINEAPPLE and KUMQUAT

1 1/2 cups PINEAPPLE, cut into chunks

1 TANGERINE, peeled, seeded, pulp removed, cut in half

3/4 cup seeded and sliced KUMQUATS (keep skin on)

1/3 cup diced tender center of CELERY

6 STRAWBERRIES

Combine first four ingredients. Top with strawberries. Serves two.

PINEAPPLE & ORANGE FRUIT DISH

1 PINEAPPLE, cut in half lengthwise

1 ORANGE, peeled and cut in chunks

1 cup STRAWBERRIES, sliced

1/2 cup diced FENNEL

MINT LEAVES

Cut skin off pineapple and dice. Mix with next three ingredients. Garnish with MINT leaves. Serves two.

STRAWBERRY & KIWI

1 basket STRAWBERRIES, quartered lengthwise

2 KIWIS, quartered and sliced

1/3 cup pre-soaked RAISINS or CURRANTS

Combine strawberries and kiwis. Sprinkle on raisins. Pour soaking water over top. Serves two.

STUFFED PEACHES

2 large, ripe PEACHES

1 cup BLACK CHERRIES or BLUEBERRIES

2 MACAROONS, crushed

APRICOT-FIG SYRUP*

Cut peaches in half and remove pit. If using black cherries, cut in half. Spoon 1/2 cup in each peach serving. Sprinkle crushed macaroons over top. Pour syrup over top.

Fruit Syrups

We must eat to live, not live to eat. Fielding

The ranks of Hygiene are filled with people who were once desperately ill and were told that medical science could do no more. By faithfully staying with Hygiene, many have made complete recoveries and have lived for decades after the doctors pronounced them: "INCURABLE!" Natural Hygiene, thus viewed, is a health care system whose time is come! Norman D. Ford, 1978.

Habit is habit and not to be flung out the window by anyone...but coaxed down the stairs, one step at a time. Mark Twain, 1870.

APRICOT-FIG SYRUP

1/2 cup dried pre-soaked APRICOTS

1/3 cup pre-soaked FIGS

Soak dried apricots and figs overnight in just enough distilled water to cover. Blend in an electric blender with just enough soaking water to puree. Pour over sweet or low-acid fruits.

BLUEBERRY APRICOT SYRUP

1/2 cup BLUEBERRIES

1/2 cup pre-soaked, chopped DRIED APRICOTS

Use just enough soaking water to puree in an electric blender. Pour over sweet or low-acid fruits. Makes enough syrup for two fruit dishes.

DATE APPLE SYRUP

6 DATES, pitted

1/2 cup DRIED APPLES

3/4 cup SWEET GRAPES, seedless

Soak dates and apples in distilled water (just enough to cover) overnight. Put grapes in blender and blend for 5 seconds. Add dates and apples. Blend. Add only enough soaking water to give you the consistency you desire. Use over sweet or low-acid fruits.

GRAPE PLUM SYRUP

1 cup SEEDLESS GRAPES

1 large PLUM, remove pit, quarter

Combine grapes and plum in blender, or nut chopper, and puree. Pour over low-acid fruit dishes.

PEACH PERSIMMON SYRUP

1 large ripe PEACH

1 medium-sized <u>ripe</u> PERSIMMON

4 large DATES

Remove pits from all fruits. Chop. Puree in an electric blender. Use on sweet or low-acid fruits.

STRAWBERRY SYRUP

With food processor, finely chop a half basket of strawberries with 3/4 cup of chopped pineapple. Mix in a tablespoon of honey if desired. Spoon over low-acid fruits. Use on low-acid fruit dishes.

Fruit Snacks

Who is strong? He that can conquer bad habits! Ben Franklin, 1770

Scientists who have studied fasting have found that a forty year old man can be fasted for 3 weeks and be restored to the physiological level of a 17 year old! Now that is remarkable! Where else can you find anything which will restore youthfulness? There is nothing else in all the realm of nature that can accomplish this as can fasting. Dr. David J. Scott, 1980.

STOP CAUSING YOUR OWN PROBLEMS! Your lifestyle is the cause. "Correct Living" is the answer for there are no cures. No running cures, bee pollen cures, no food cures.

ALMOND OATMEAL COOKIES

1 cup ALMOND BUTTER

1 tablespoon HONEY

3/4 cup OATMEAL

1/2 cup DISTILLED WATER

1/2 cup RAISINS

1/2 cup chopped ALMONDS

1/2 teaspoon VANILLA

Bring almond butter to room temperature for 20 minutes. Soak oatmeal with water. Let stand 5 minutes. Combine all ingredients in a small bowl using a wooden spoon. Use a tablespoon to scoop out enough for one cookie. Place on greased cookie sheet. Press each cookie with the tines of a fork. Refrigerate for one hour before serving.

FRUIT FUDGE SQUARES

2 cups OATMEAL

1/2 cup SOY FLOUR

1 1/2 cup finely ground SUNFLOWER SEEDS

2 tablespoons HONEY

4 tablespoons ALMOND OIL

1 1/2 cups pre-soaked APRICOTS

1/2 cup CURRANTS

3/4 cup ground ALMONDS or PECANS

Mix first five ingredients together. Divide in half. Sprinkle half the mixture in a glass baking dish and press to cover bottom of dish. Mix next three ingredients together. Spread mixture on top. Sprinkle other half of dry mixture on top and press down. Chill for 1 hour. Cut in squares.

FRUIT-NUT BONBONS

1/2 cup pre-soaked RAISINS

3/4 cup fresh or pre-soaked FIGS

1/2 cup dried pre-soaked APRICOTS

3/4 cup WALNUTS, chopped small

1 cup grated COCONUT

Combine first three ingredients in blender and grind together using just enough of the soaking water to make it chunky. Put in bowl and mix in walnut thoroughly with your hands. Shape into small balls (about the size of walnuts). Roll in coconut. Store in refrigerator.

FRUIT NUT ROLL

Use assortment of dried fruits like apricots, prunes, figs, dates, apple, and papaya. Soak in distilled water overnight in refrigerator. Use only enough water to cover them. Use an electric chopper to make a nut meal from walnut, or pecans, or cashews. Roll the fruit in the nut meal. Store in refrigerator.

PECAN-RAISIN BALLS

1 lb. PECANS

1/4 cup ROLLED OATS

10 DATES, pitted

2 tablespoons raw TAHINI

1 teaspoon CINNAMON

1 teaspoon VANILLA EXTRACT

1 cup pre-soaked RAISINS, drained on a cloth dish towel.

Finely grind pecans and oats in food processor, using the "S" blade. Spoon into mixing bowl and set aside. Put dates, tahini, cinnamon and vanilla into processor and blend into a paste. Mix paste into pecan-oat mixture. Add raisins and blend well. Roll mixture into small balls. Makes about 10 balls.

STUFFED DATES

1/4 pound EMPRESS DATES, pitted

ALMOND or PECAN BUTTER

1/2 cup ALMOND or PECAN meal

Whole ALMONDS and PECANS

Slit dates open. Stuff with nut butter. Insert one nut in each date. Sprinkle with meal. Store in refrigerator.

SUNFLOWER-RAISIN COOKIES

3 cups soaked SUNFLOWER SEEDS

1 cup ALMOND BUTTER

1 cup organic, pre-soaked RAISINS

1 cup chopped, dried, pre-soaked APRICOTS

1 tablespoon real VANILLA, optional

1/2 teaspoon CINNAMON, optional

Pre-soak RAISINS and APRICOTS overnight in distilled water. When preparing cookies, drain well. Blend all ingredients in food processor to a nutty consistency. Roll in small balls and flatten out 1/4" thick. Can dehydrate to desired crispness, or cover and refrigerate for 1 hour.

Dips

We are the living graves of murdered beasts, slaughtered to satisfy our appetites...George Bernard Shaw, 1940.

Physical, mental, and moral integrity constitute our most precious possessions - a balanced, sound mind in a balanced, sound body. We have a moral obligation to ourselves, dear ones, society, posterity, and our Maker to strive for optimum health through obedience to natural laws governing health. The physical, mental, and moral health of the people of any nation is more important than its "gross national product." Harry Kaplan, 1984.

It is a requisite that men and women should be content with little and accustom ourselves to eat no more than is absolutely necessary to support life - remember that all excess causes disease and leads to death. Luigi Coronado, 1458 - 1560.

CARROT & JICAMA DIP

1/2 medium-sized CUCUMBER, pealed and chopped

2 tablespoons LIME JUICE

1 cup finely shredded CARROT

1 cup finely grated JICAMA

1/4 cup coarsely ground SUNFLOWER SEEDS

1/2 teaspoon finely chopped fresh DILL

Liquefy cucumber and lime juice in an electric blender. Add remaining ingredients and grind.

CHICK PEA DIP

1 cup CHICK PEA SPROUTS

2 tablespoons LIME JUICE

1 clove GARLIC, minced

1 VEGETABLE BOUILLON, crushed

2 tablespoons CHIVES, minced

Grind the chick pea sprouts very finely in a blender. Transfer to small bowl. Add lime, garlic and bouillon and mix well. Sprinkle with chives.

GARBANZO DIP

3/4 cup dry GARBANZO BEANS (See "How to pre-soak" in Introduction, page 12).

1 small chopped TOMATILLO

2 tablespoons "Mild" LIQUID SOY

1 small GARLIC clove, chopped

1/8 cup WATERCRESS, chopped

1/4 cup chopped SESAME SEEDS

1/2 teaspoon DILL SEED

Rinse garbanzo beans after soaking. Grate in food processor. Put liquid soy, tomatillo, garlic, garbanzos in blender in order given. Grind until chunky. Put in bowl and mix in remaining ingredients. Use with vegetable dippers.

*This dish requires soaking of garbanzo beans two days in advance.

GUACAMOLE

2 ripe HAAS AVOCADOS

1 tablespoon LEMON or LIME JUICE

1 small TOMATILLO, finely diced

2 tablespoons mild SALSA or DAIKON*

2 tablespoons chopped BLACK OLIVES

small clove GARLIC, minced (optional)

Cut avocados in half lengthwise. Remove seeds and, cut thin slices in both directions while still in skin. Scoop out meat. Sprinkle with lemon and smash with a fork in small bowl. Add tomatillo and mix together. Blend in remaining ingredients. Serve with vegetable dippers.

*If you use the daikon instead of the salsa, add 1 medium-sized diced PLUM TOMATO

KOHLRABI ITALIENNE

6 to 8 KOHLRABIES

DIP

4 tablespoons TOMATO PASTE

1 tablespoon OLIVE OIL

1 small clove GARLIC, minced

1/2 small CUCUMBER, peeled, diced

6 PLUM TOMATOES, chopped small

3 tablespoons ground SESAME SEEDS

2 tablespoons chopped OLIVES

Peel the kohlrabies. Slice lengthwise. Whip tomato paste and olive oil. Blend in garlic, cucumber, tomatoes, seeds, olives. If necessary, add water very gradually.

ITALIAN PESTO

3/4 cup PINE NUTS (also called pignolia nuts)

1 handful fresh BASIL LEAVES

2 or 3 1" long, fresh OREGANO LEAVES

1/3 cup VIRGIN OLIVE OIL

1 small GARLIC clove, minced

Grind nuts in blender. Slowly add oil. Remove stalks from herbs. Blend in herbs and garlic.

MEXICAN SALSA

Juice of half LIME

1 cup ripe TOMATOES, finely diced

1 YELLOW PEPPER, finely diced

1/2 cup finely diced, tender center of CELERY

2 small TOMATILLOS, diced

1 teaspoon minced fresh GINGER ROOT

Mix all thoroughly.

MOCK TUNA DIP

1/2 cup ground SESAME SEEDS

1 tablespoon KELP

1/2 cup finely diced CELERY

3/4 cup ground MUNG & LENTIL SPROUTS

Juice from 1/2 PINK GRAPEFRUIT

Combine all ingredients in a bowl except the grapefruit juice. Slowly pour the amount needed for the consistency you want.

Vegetable Drinks

We must change our negative thoughts and feelings - for that is what is killing us! If we forgive the past, drop negative thoughts, stop being victims - we drop our disease, as well. For the mechanism that holds on to negative thoughts and feelings is the same one that holds onto disease. Sondra Ray, 1980.

Man is the only animal that must have as many as 30 different foods at one sitting. Dr. John Brosious, 1969.

The secret to getting rid of old, destructive habits lies in loving and respecting yourself so much that you do not succumb to the addictive stimulation that is so powerfully projected to make us puppets on the strings of Madison Avenue manipulators.
Jo Willard, 1982.

VEGETABLE DRINKS

Use only fresh, ripe fruits and vegetables, preferably organically grown. If regular supermarket quality produce is used, they should be washed carefully. See "How to Clean Vegetables" in Introduction, page 13.

Make only the amount of juice that will be used immediately. In storage, even under refrigeration, raw juices oxidize rapidly and lose their medicinal value after 10 minutes.

Sweet juices such as carrot, beet, grape, apple or pear juice, should be diluted with water 50-50, or mixed with other, less sweet juices.

Never mix fruit and vegetable juices together. The combining of these two classes of foods impairs digestion and assimilation, resulting in gas with only partial assimilation of nutrients.

Drink vegetable or fruit juices between meals or one hour before meals but never with meals.

Drink juices slowly, and salivate well.

Combine the following groups in juicer.

2 or 3 TOMATOES, 1 CELERY stalk, 1 BEET, 1 small CUCUMBER.

2 or 3 TOMATOES, 1 CELERY stalk, 1 BEET, 1 small CUCUMBER, 1 cup CABBAGE.

Any green tops such as, PARSLEY, SPINACH, KALE, SWISS CHARD, TURNIP TOPS, RADISH TOPS, mixed with CARROT, TOMATO, STRING BEANS.

HEAD LETTUCE, CARROTS, STRING BEANS, BELL PEPPERS.

2 or 3 TOMATOES, 1 CELERY stalk, 2" bottom length of DAIKON.

3 to 4 CARROTS, 1 small JICAMA, 1 small TOMATILLO, 1/2 cup PARSLEY.

1 large CUCUMBER, 1 large BEET, 1 cup SPROUTS, handful STRING BEANS.

2 or 3 TOMATOES, 1/2 cup CORN, 1 or 2 PARSNIPS, fresh BASIL.

TOMATO, CELERY, GREEN PEPPER, CUCUMBER, one tablespoon SOY or LEMON JUICE, 1 teaspoon CELERY SEED.

1/4 cup of sprouted SUNFLOWER SEEDS can be added to each group for a creamy drink.

Soups

The one sure road to better nutrition and better health is first to fast. Let your body do its professional and expert job of nourishing you during the fast, and then, with your taste buds cleansed of the false craving for junk, you will readily embrace the fresh fruits, vegetables, nuts and seeds and you can finally break away from the junk. Seneca, 62 A.D.

Man lives on one-fourth of what he eats. On the other three-fourths lives his doctor. Inscription on an Egyptian pyramid, 3800 B.C.

Should a man, when ill, continue to eat the same amounts as when in health, he would surely die; while were he to eat more, he would surely die all the sooner. For his natural powers, already oppressed with sickness, would thereby be burdened with sickness, would thereby be burdened beyond endurance, having had forced upon them a quantity of food greater than they could support under the circumstances. A reduced quantity of food is, in my opinion, all that is required to sustain the individual into a long life. Luigi Coronado, 1458 - 1560.

ASPARAGUS SOUP

1 cup DRINKING WATER

ASPARAGUS for two, sliced 1" (set aside tips)

1 cup grated JICAMA

1 CELERY stalk, cut in 1" lengths

1/2 cup finely diced, CELERY

1/3 cup WATERCRESS, chopped

1/2 cup WALNUTS, chopped

Use drinking water to steam asparagus for 4 minutes (See "Steaming Instructions" on page 12). Use same water to liquefy jicama and celery in electric blender (add only enough water as necessary). Add asparagus and blend again. Transfer to large bowl. Mix in watercress. Ladle into individual bowls. Lightly season. Garnish with asparagus tips and walnuts.

AVOCADO & CAULIFLOWER SOUP

3 cups CAULIFLOWER florets

1 medium to large HAAS AVOCADO

1 cup DRINKING WATER

1 cup ALFALFA SPROUTS, cut in thirds

1 teaspoon fresh, minced BASIL LEAF

Your choice of the following as a garnish, PEAS, or CORN, or PLUM TOMATOES, diced, or CARROT, grated

Steam cauliflower 5 minutes with drinking water. Remove from heat and transfer to covered bowl. Seed avocado, and cut thin slices in both directions while still in skin. Remove pulp from skin. Place both in blender with steaming water. Add more water as necessary. Blend until smooth. Pour into soup dishes. Add sprouts and basil. Garnish with your choice of vegetable.

AVOCADO & TOMATO SOUP

2 cups TOMATO JUICE from fresh tomatoes made in blender

1 small TOMATILLO, chopped

1 heaping tablespoon ALMOND BUTTER

1 ripe HAAS AVOCADO

1 teaspoon fresh, minced BASIL LEAF

Seed avocado, and cut thin slices in both directions while still in skin. Remove pulp with a tablespoon. Combine all ingredients except basil in an electric blender in order given. Blend until smooth. Serve at room temperature or chill. Sprinkle with basil. Serves two.

BARLEY CARROT SOUP*

3/4 cup BARLEY

1 cup DRINKING WATER

2 cups CARROT JUICE

1/2 cup chopped CELERY

2 tablespoons minced DAIKON

1/2 cup chopped PARSLEY

Soak barley overnight in distilled water. Rinse under hot water. Drain well. Combine all ingredients. Serves two. Note: Save the carrot pulp for "Vege Burgers" recipe if making the same day.

*This dish requires soaking barley overnight.

BROCCOLI ZUCCHINI SOUP

1 small head BROCCOLI

2 cups chopped ZUCCHINI

1 cup DISTILLED WATER

1/2 cup diced CELERY

1/2 small RED PEPPER, diced

1/3 cup PINE NUTS

1 teaspoon fresh, minced OREGANO

Cut broccoli into florets. Steam only four minutes. (See "Steaming Instructions" on page 12). Blend broccoli, zucchini and steaming water in blender until smooth. Add more water as necessary. Pour in soup dishes. Mix in celery, pepper and pine nuts. Sprinkle with oregano. Serves two.

CAULIFLOWER & CORN SOUP

CAULIFLOWER florets for two

1 1/4 cups drinking WATER

1 medium grated PARSNIP

2 ears of CORN, kerneled (See "How to Kernel" on page 13)

1/2 teaspoon DILL SEED

1/4 cup chopped WATERCRESS

Steam cauliflower 5 minutes (See "Steaming Instructions" on page 12). Puree the cauliflower, parsnip, and steaming water in electric blender until smooth. Add more water if necessary. Remove from blender and add corn and dill. Garnish with watercress. Chill if desired. Serves two.

CHICK PEAS & TOMATO SOUP*

1/2 cup dry CHICK PEAS

2 cups TOMATO JUICE from fresh tomatoes made in blender

1/2 cup ground NUTS (walnuts, almonds, or pecans)

1/2 cup diced CELERY

WATERCRESS

Soak chick peas in distilled water overnight. (See "How to Soak Garbanzo Beans" on page 12). Rinse chick peas after they are soaked. Drain well. Combine chick peas and tomato in electric blender and liquefy. Pour in soup bowls. Mix in nuts and celery. Garnish with watercress. Serve at room temperature or chilled. Serves two.

*This dish requires soaking chick peas for two days.

COLD AVOCADO SOUP

1 and 1/2 HAAS AVOCADO

1 half AVOCADO, pitted, removed from skin, diced (set aside)

3/4 medium CUCUMBER, chopped

1/4 CUCUMBER, diced small (set aside)

2 large, ripe TOMATOES, quartered

1/4 cup chopped WATERCRESS

Remove pit from avocado. Cut thin slices in both directions while still in skin. Remove pulp with a tablespoon. Whirl tomatoes, avocado and cucumber in blender until smooth. Pour into bowls. Stir in avocado and cucumber. Chill if desired. Garnish with watercress. Serves two.

COOL TOMATO SOUP

2 cups freshly made TOMATO JUICE

1 1/2 medium CUCUMBERS, peeled, chopped

1/2 medium CUCUMBER, peeled, diced (set aside)

1 cup ALFALFA SPROUTS, cut in thirds

1 small GREEN BELL PEPPER, finely diced

1 teaspoon fresh, minced BASIL LEAVES or OREGANO LEAVES

1/4 cup WATERCRESS, chopped

Puree tomatoes and chopped cucumbers. Pour mixture into large bowl. Add next four ingredients. Pour in individual bowls.

Garnish with watercress. Serves two.

CORN CHOWDER

1 to 1 1/2 cups drinking WATER

1 rib of CELERY, chopped in 1" lengths

1 cup shredded JICAMA

2 medium PARSNIPS, shredded

2 ears of CORN, kerneled (See "How to Kernel" on page 13)

1 ear of CORN, kerneled (set aside)

1/2 cup finely diced, tender rib of CELERY

1/2 teaspoon ANISE

6 WALNUTS, chopped

1/4 cup minced PARSLEY

Place half the amount of celery, jicama, parsnip and corn in electric blender with just enough water to blend. Pour into large bowl. Blend other half. Mix in corn, celery and anise. Ladle into individual bowls. Garnish with walnuts and parsley. serves two.

CREAM OF SPINACH SOUP

2 cups chopped, fresh SPINACH

1 1/2 cups chopped ZUCCHINI

1 1/2 cups DRINKING WATER

2 tablespoons diced DAIKON

1 tablespoon finely cut FRESH KELP

1/2 cup diced RED BELL PEPPER

Cut off stems from spinach. Blend first five ingredients in blender. Pour into soup bowls. Sprinkle with pepper. Serves two.

CREAMY CARROT & AVOCADO SOUP

3 cups fresh CARROT JUICE

1 large HAAS AVOCADO

handful ALFALFA SPROUTS, cut in thirds

small sprig CILANTRO, leaves only

Make carrot juice. Cut avocado in half. Remove pit. Cut thin slices in both directions while still in skin. Keep halves separated. Place carrot juice and one half avocado in blender. Blend until smooth. Pour into individual soup bowls. Mix other half of avocado and sprouts with soup. Add cilantro. Note: Cilantro leaves should never be cut.

GREEN PEA SOUP

1 large HAAS AVOCADO, removed from skin, pitted, chopped

1 1/2 cups fresh PEAS

1 medium ZUCCHINI, chopped

1 1/4 cups distilled WATER

2 tablespoons minced DAIKON (optional)

1 CARROT, grated

1/2 teaspoon DILL SEED

2 sprigs PARSLEY, chopped

Blend avocado, peas, zucchini, water (use more if necessary), and daikon in blender until creamy. Mix in carrots and dill. Sprinkle with parsley. Serves two.

LIFE FORCE SOUP

4 large CARROTS, grated

1 cup grated JICAMA

1 cup PARSLEY

1/2 bunch SPINACH (See "How to Wash" on page 12)

2 large TOMATOES, quartered

1 cup ALFALFA SPROUTS

Puree all ingredients in electric blender until smooth. Chill or serve immediately. Serves two.

PARSNIP SOUP

2 cups grated PARSNIPS

1 1/2 cups DRINKING WATER

1 ear CORN, kerneled (See "How to Kernel Corn" on page 13)

1 medium CARROT, finely grated

1 sprig PARSLEY, minced

1/2 teaspoon ANISE

Blend parsnips and water in blender at high speed for 30 seconds. Add anise. Blend for 3 seconds. Pour into soup bowls. Mix in corn and carrot. Garnish with parsley. Serves two.

RAW BORSCHT

4 small young BEETS, chopped

1/4 head medium CABBAGE, sliced and chopped

1 cup CARROT JUICE, made fresh in juicer

1 small <u>fresh</u> JICAMA, chopped in 1" squares 1 CELERY rib and leaves, chopped

1 to 1 1/2 cups DRINKING WATER

1/4 cup chopped WATERCRESS

Liquefy first six vegetables a bit at a time using water as necessary in electric blender. Pour into individual bowls. Add caraway. Garnish with watercress. Serves two.

Note: Always use fresh jicama in making soup. Old jicama is dry. Also, save carrot pulp for "Vege Burgers" recipe if you are making it the same day.

SWEET POTATO SOUP

1 to 1 1/2 cups DRINKING WATER

3 cups grated, SWEET POTATOES or YAMS

1 medium PARSNIP, grated

1/2 cup diced, FENNEL

SUNFLOWER SPROUTS

Place sweet potatoes and parsnips in an electric blender with just enough water to liquefy. Pour mixture in soup bowls. Blend in fennel. Sprinkle with sprouts in center. Serves two.

TOMATO VEGETABLE SOUP

3 cups freshly made TOMATO JUICE

1 ear CORN, kerneled (See "How to Kernel" on page 13)

3/4 cup fresh PEAS

1/2 cup diced, CELERY

1 teaspoon fresh, minced BASIL LEAVES

1/3 cup WATERCRESS

6 WALNUTS, chopped

Mix above ingredients in large bowl. Ladle into individual soup bowls. Garnish with nuts and watercress. Serve immediately. Serves two.

TOMATO ZUCCHINI SOUP

3 or 4 large TOMATOES, quartered

1 medium ZUCCHINI, grated

1/2 cup chopped WALNUTS

1/2 cup diced tender rib of CELERY

2 tablespoons grated DAIKON

3/4 cup SWEET BABY PEAS

Liquefy tomatoes, zucchini and walnuts in an electric blender. Chill if desired. Pour into bowls and sprinkle with celery, daikon and peas. Serves two.

ZUCCHINI & PEA SOUP

3 medium ZUCCHINI, grated (should make 3 to 3 1/2 cups)

2 cups fresh PEAS

1 to 1 1/2 cups DRINKING WATER

2 tablespoons diced DAIKON

1/2 cup diced CELERY

1 teaspoon fresh, minced BASIL LEAVES

Blend first four ingredients in blender until smooth. Use only enough water for a soupy consistency. Pour into soup bowls. Mix in celery and basil. Serves two.

Dressings

If the medical professionals courageously popularized the fast among their patients, there would be infinitely less suffering than there is now. That many would be saved who now die through the drug and feeding treatment is a certainty. Ghandi, 1945.

When various cells of the body are overloaded with the toxic residues of drugs and chemically harmful foods or beverages or from the effects of overeating or wrong food combinations, sleep difficulties often result. Or, if the body is so depleted from over-activity during the day, it is also likely to tell of its woes by producing a night of sleeplessness. To avoid this problem, Hygienists strongly recommend a short nap or rest period during the day for relaxation and replenishment. Tomar Kent 1979.

(Note: When preparing most of these recipes, it may be necessary to take a firm grip on the top and bottom of the blender and shake the contents so they will hit the blade. It's not necessary to lift it off the counter).

AVOCADO TOMATILLO DRESSING

1 tablespoon LIQUID SOY

1 medium-small TOMATILLO, chopped

1/2 medium CUCUMBER, chopped

1 tablespoon diced DAIKON

1 large HAAS AVOCADO

1/4 to 1/2 teaspoon DILL

Cut avocado in half. Remove pit. Cut thin slices in both directions while still in skin. Remove pulp with tablespoon. Blend soy, tomatillo, cucumber and daikon in electric blender. Add avocado. Blend until creamy. Add dill to taste.

AVOCADO TOMATO DRESSING

1 large, ripe TOMATO, chopped

1 large HAAS AVOCADO

1/2 medium, small CUCUMBER, peeled, chopped

1 teaspoon minced, OREGANO

Cut avocado in half. Remove pit. Cut thin slices in both directions while still in skin. Remove pulp with tablespoon. Blend all ingredients in electric blender until smooth.

CARROT CELERY DRESSING

1 cup CARROTS, shredded

2 tender ribs of CELERY, chopped

1/2 medium CUCUMBER, peeled, chopped

2 tablespoons LIQUID SOY

1/4 cup ground ALMONDS

Peel carrots. Use fresh (has tops on) carrots. Old carrots are dry. Place all ingredients in blender in the following order: soy, cucumber, celery, carrots and almonds. Blend until smooth.

CASHEW DRESSING

CASHEW BUTTER

DISTILLED WATER

LIME JUICE

Mix to taste and consistency desired using electric blender.

CREAMY CELERY DRESSING

3/4 cup chopped CELERY

1/2 medium CUCUMBER, peeled, chopped

1/4 cup ground WALNUTS

2 to 3 tablespoons LIQUID SOY

Combine ingredients in electric blender. Blend until creamy.

CREAMY CUCUMBER DRESSING

Juice from 1/2 PINK GRAPEFRUIT or medium-small TOMATILLO, chopped
1 medium CUCUMBER, peeled, chopped
1/2 cup ground WALNUTS

Combine all ingredients in electric blender. Blend until smooth.

CREAMY TOMATO DRESSING

2 cups chopped TOMATOES
1/2 cup ground WALNUTS
2 sprigs fresh PARSLEY

Combine ingredients in an electric blender. Blend until smooth.

CUCUMBER DRESSING

1 medium CUCUMBER, peeled, chopped
1 medium-small TOMATILLO, chopped
2 tender ribs CELERY, chopped

Combine ingredients in blender. Blend until smooth.

CUCUMBER KELP DRESSING

1 tablespoon "Mild" LIQUID SOY

1 medium CUCUMBER, peeled, chopped

1" long DAIKON, grated or 1 GARLIC CLOVE, diced

1 10" long strip, dried KELP

Cut kelp into 1/2" long pieces using kitchen shears. Put all ingredients in blender in order shown. Blend until smooth.

GARBANZO CUCUMBER DRESSING*

Juice from 1/2 PINK GRAPEFRUIT or 1 small TOMATILLO, chopped

1 rib of CELERY, chopped

1/2 medium CUCUMBER, chopped

3/4 cup GARBANZO BEANS (See "How to Soak Garbanzo Beans" on page 12).

Rinse soaked beans. Drain well. Combine ingredients in electric blender. Blend until smooth.

*This recipe requires soaking of garbanzo beans for two days.

TOMATO CUCUMBER DRESSING

2 large TOMATOES, chopped

1/2 medium CUCUMBER, peeled, chop?ed

1 rib of CELERY, chopped

3 tablespoons finely grated DAIKON

1 tablespoon, fresh minced OREGANO LEAF

Combine all ingredients in electric blender until smooth.

Main Dishes

*Tell me what you eat and I'll tell you what you are. Anthelme Brilat-Savarin
(1825)*

APPLACADO SALAD

2 red-skinned APPLES, cored, diced

2 tablespoons LEMON JUICE

2 HAAS AVOCADOS, pitted, chopped.

1/2 cup diced tender center of CELERY

ALFALFA SPROUTS, cut in half

1/2 teaspoon CINNAMON

SNOWPEAS, handful

LETTUCE

CASHEW DRESSING*

Prepare a bed of lettuce. Sprinkle lemon juice on apples to prevent discoloration. It is not necessary to remove skin from avocado to dice or chop. Cut avocado in half. Remove pit. Cut thin lines in both directions. Scoop out pulp with tablespoon. Combine apples, avocados, celery, sprouts, and cinnamon. Scoop mixture on a head of lettuce toward the center. Cut stem and peel string of snowpeas. Place in a pinwheel design around the dish. Pour dressing over top. Serves two.

ASPARAGUS & RUTABAGA

ASPARAGUS for two

1 small RUTABAGA, grated

2 stems BOK CHOY, sliced thin diagonally

1 small RED PEPPER, diced

CASHEW DRESSING*

Cut asparagus in bite-size lengths. Steam for 3 minutes. Follow steaming instructions in "How to Steam" on page 12. Combine first four ingredients. Place on individual plates. Pour dressing over top.

AVOCADO & CAULIFLOWER

SPINACH for two, broken in bite-size pieces

CAULIFLOWER florets, for two, sliced

8 CHERRY TOMATOES, quartered

3/4 cup fresh PEAS

1 ear CORN, kerneled

2 ripe HAAS AVOCADOS

1 fresh BASIL, minced

CREAMY CELERY DRESSING*

Place spinach on plate. Refrigerate. It is not necessary to remove skin from avocado to dice or chop. Cut avocado in half. Remove pit. Cut thin lines in both directions. Remove pulp with tablespoon. Combine cauliflower, tomatoes, peas, avocado, corn and basil in a bowl. Refrigerate while making dressing. Scoop mixture on spinach. Pour dressing over top.

AVOCADO & ZUCCHINI

2 medium small ZUCCHINI, unpeeled, grated

1 small YELLOW BELL PEPPER, diced

2 ripe HAAS AVOCADOS

1/3 cup black, sliced OLIVES

SALAD GREENS

TOMATILLO CUCUMBER DRESSING*

Prepare a bed of greens. It is not necessary to remove skin from avocado to dice or chop. Cut avocado in half. Remove pit. Cut thin lines in both directions. Remove pulp with tablespoon. Combine first four ingredients. Scoop mixture on greens. Pour dressing over top. Serves two.

BARLEY & STRING BEANS*

1 cup uncooked BARLEY

1 1/2 cups DISTILLED WATER

STRING BEANS for 2, cut 1" lengths

1 small HAAS AVOCADO

1 cup SUNFLOWER or ALFALFA SPROUTS

CARROT CELERY DRESSING*

Cover barley with distilled water and soak overnight. Change water in morning.

Rinse barley under hot water in sieve. Drain well. Cut avocado in half. Remove pit. Slice thin lines in both directions while still in skin. Remove pulp with tablespoon. Combine barley with beans, avocado and sprouts. Pour dressing over top. Serves two.

*Note: This dish requires overnight soaking of barley.

BEET & JICAMA

4 small, young BEETS, cut in julienne style

1 cup grated JICAMA

4 BRUSSELS SPROUTS, sliced thin. Separate layers.

1/3 cup diced, tender rib of CELERY

1/3 cup sliced OLIVES

TOMATILLO CUCUMBER DRESSING*

Combine first 4 ingredients. Refrigerate while making dressing. Pour dressing over top. Garnish with olives. Serves two.

98

BROCCOLI & CARROT

BROCCOLI for two, cut in florets
1 cup grated CARROTS
1 cup ALFALFA SPROUTS, cut in half
2 tablespoons DAIKON
1/2 teaspoon DILL SEED
TOMATILLO CUCUMBER DRESSING*
1/3 cup sliced OLIVES
LETTUCE

Combine first five ingredients. Scoop on a bed of lettuce. Pour dressing over top. Garnish with olives. Serves two.

BROCCOLI & ZUCCHINI

BROCCOLI florets for two
1 ZUCCHINI, grated
1 medium size RED BELL PEPPER, diced
1 cup BEAN SPROUTS
1 medium CUCUMBER, peeled, chopped
3 tablespoons "Mild" LIQUID SOY
1 teaspoon DILL SEED
1/4 cup SLICED OLIVES

Combine first four ingredients. Refrigerate while making dressing. Put soy, cucumber, dill in blender and liquefy. Pour over mixture. Garnish with olives. Serves two.

BROCCOLI & BOK CHOY with TOMATO

BROCCOLI florets for 2
2 BOK CHOY STEMS, include tops, cut length-wise, slivered diagonally
2 medium TOMATOES, chopped
1 cup ALFALFA SPROUTS
1/3 cup chopped WALNUTS
AVOCADO TOMATILLO DRESSING*

Combine first five ingredients, Pour dressing over top. Garnish with walnuts. Serves two.

BRUSSELS SPROUTS & BELL PEPPER

1/2 pound BRUSSELS SPROUTS, sliced thin. Separate layers.
1 small RED BELL PEPPER, finely diced
1 cup grated PARSNIP
3/4 cup fresh PEAS
1 cup SUNFLOWER SPROUTS, cut in half
1/2 teaspoon CARAWAY SEED
TOMATILLO CUCUMBER DRESSING*
1/4 cup sliced OLIVES

Combine first six ingredients. Pour dressing over top. Garnish with olives. Serves two.

CABBAGE SLAW SALAD

Shredded green CABBAGE for two

3/4 cup grated CARROTS

1 green BELL PEPPER, finely diced

3/4 cup fresh or frozen CORN

3 tablespoons grated DAIKON

1 teaspoon CARAWAY SEED

AVOCADO TOMATILLO DRESSING*

1/2 cup sliced OLIVES

Combine first six ingredients. Pour dressing over top. Garnish with olives. Can be served immediately or chilled. Chill for 20 minutes in a covered casserole dish or cover with plastic wrap. Serves two.

CARROT & APPLE SALAD

1 cup grated CARROTS

4 BRUSSELS SPROUTS, cut in half, sliced thin

1 medium PARSNIP, grated

1/2 cup pre-soaked, chopped RAISINS

1 teaspoon ANISE

2 yellow-skinned APPLES, cored, diced

2 tablespoons LEMON JUICE

CASHEW DRESSING*

1/4 cup WATERCRESS, chopped

1 head BOSTON LETTUCE

Combine first five ingredients. Cut apple and sprinkle with lemon juice to prevent discoloration. Mix with other five ingredients. Scoop mixture on bed of lettuce. Pour dressing over top. Garnish with watercress. Serves two.

CARROT SALAD

2 cups grated CARROTS

1 cup grated JICAMA

2 ears of CORN, kerneled

4 BRUSSELS SPROUTS, sliced thin

1 cup ALFALFA SPROUTS, cut in half

CREAMY CUCUMBER DRESSING*

1/2 cup chopped OLIVES

LETTUCE

Prepare a bed of lettuce. Combine first five ingredients. Scoop onto lettuce. Pour dressing over top. Garnish with olives. Serves two.

CARROT-NUT PATTIES

2 cups grated CARROTS

1/4 cup SESAME SEED, ground

1/4 cup SUNFLOWER SEED, ground

2 tablespoons minced DAIKON

3 tablespoons finely chopped CELERY

CREAMY CELERY DRESSING*

SALAD GREENS

Prepare a bed of greens. Combine first five ingredients. Form into patties and place on greens. Pour dressing over top. Serves two.

CARROT OATMEAL PATTIES

1 cup OATMEAL

1/2 cup DRINKING WATER

1 1/2 cups grated CARROTS

2 tablespoons minced DAIKON

1/2 cup diced CELERY

1/3 cup chopped CASHEWS

CASHEW DRESSING*

SALAD GREENS

Soak oatmeal with water for five minutes. Mix with fork several times. Should be moist not mushy. Prepare a bed of greens. Combine next four ingredients with oatmeal. Mix thoroughly. Form into patties. Place on bed of greens. Pour dressing over top.

CAULIFLOWER & SPINACH CASSEROLE

CAULIFLOWER florets, for two

1/2 bunch SPINACH (see "How to wash Spinach," on page 12)

2 ears of CORN, kerneled

1 cup SUNFLOWER SPROUTS

1 tablespoon fresh, minced BASIL

CREAMY TOMATO DRESSING*

1/2 cup sliced OLIVES

Cut cauliflower in bite-size pieces. Brake spinach into bite sized pieces. Combine first four ingredients. Pour dressing over top. Garnish with olives. Serves two.

GREEN BEANS & ZUCCHINI

GREEN BEANS for 2, cut 1"

1 medium ZUCCHINI, grated

1 cup CARROTS, grated

1 ear CORN, kerneled

CARROT CELERY DRESSING*

SALAD GREENS

Prepare a bed of greens. Combine first four ingredients. Scoop onto greens. Pour dressing over top. Serves two.

JICAMA & PEAS

2 cups grated JICAMA

1/3 cup YELLOW BELL PEPPER, diced

2 tablespoons minced DAIKON

1/3 cup diced, tender center of CELERY

1/8 cup chopped PARSLEY

4 CHERRY TOMATOES, quartered

1 cup fresh PEAS

CREAMY CUCUMBER DRESSING*

ROMAINE lettuce

6 STUFFED GREEN OLIVES

Combine the first six ingredients. Add peas and mix gently. Add only enough dressing to make mixture moist. Chill. Form into individual mounds. Place on bed of lettuce greens. Pour the rest of the dressing on top. Garnish with olives. Serves two.

KIDNEY BEANS & GREEN PEPPER*

3/4 cup dry RED KIDNEY BEANS

1 1/2 cups DISTILLED WATER

1 GREEN BELL PEPPER, diced

1 small RUTABAGA or TURNIP, grated

2 cups SUNFLOWER SPROUTS

GARBANZO CUCUMBER DRESSING*

*(calls for pre-soaked garbanzo beans)

2 tablespoons SLICED OLIVES

LETTUCE

Use water to soak kidney beans overnight. Combine with next three ingredients. Make a bed of lettuce. Scoop mixture over greens. Pour dressing over top. Garnish with olives. Serves two. Note: Not all kidney beans plump up from soaking. Remove any small, bright red beans.

OATMEAL BURGERS

3/4 cup OATMEAL

1/2 cup DRINKING WATER

1 cup WHEAT SPROUTS, coarsely ground

1/3 cup chopped GREEN PEPPER

1 TOMATO, finely chopped

2 tablespoons minced DAIKON

1 or 2 tender center CELERY ribs, diced

2 tablespoons minced PARSLEY

SALAD GREENS

MEXICAN SALSA*

Soak oatmeal in water for 5 minutes. Combine next six ingredients. Mix thoroughly. Shape into patties. Place on a bed of greens. Spoon salsa over top.

PARSNIPS & OKRA with TOMATOES

2 medium PARSNIPS, grated

8 OKRAS, cut bite size

4 PLUM TOMATOES, diced

CASHEW DRESSING*

ALFALFA SPROUTS

SALAD GREENS

Prepare bed of greens. Cut away hard stringy edges on okra, and scrape skin. Combine parsnip, okra and tomatoes. Scoop onto greens. Pour dressing over top. Garnish with sprouts. Serves two.

PEAS & RUTABAGA

1 cup fresh PEAS

1 small RUTABAGA, peeled and finely grated

1 CUCUMBER, peeled, diced

1 cup ALFALFA SPROUTS, cut in half

1/2 teaspoon CARAWAY

SALAD GREENS

TOMATILLO CUCUMBER DRESSING*

2 tablespoons PINE NUTS

Combine first five ingredients. Scoop onto bed of lettuce. Pour dressing over top. Garnish with pine nuts. Serves two.

PEAS & SAVOY CABBAGE

Shredded SAVOY CABBAGE for two

1 1/2 cups fresh PEAS

1 medium CUCUMBER, diced

1 YELLOW BELL PEPPER, diced

1/2 to 1 teaspoon DILL SEED

AVOCADO DRESSING*

1/2 cup SLICED OLIVES

Combine first five ingredients. Pour dressing over top. Garnish with olives. Serves two.

POTATO SALAD

Small RED or NEW WHITE POTATOES for two

DISTILLED WATER for soaking

JUICE from 1/2 LEMON

1/2 large RED BELL PEPPER, diced

1/2 large YELLOW BELL PEPPER, diced

1/2 cup minced tender center CELERY

3 tablespoons minced DAIKON

1 spring PARSLEY, minced

1/2 teaspoon DILL SEED

1 teaspoon powdered KELP

CUCUMBER DRESSING*

Scrub potatoes well. Peel if desired. Cut potatoes in julienne style. If not bite-sized, cut in half. Cover potatoes in distilled water. Add lemon juice and let soak for 30 minutes to release starch, making them digestible. Drain potatoes and rinse well in another bowl of distilled water. Dry on a clean, cloth towel. Mix with all dry ingredients. Pour dressing over top. Mix. Refrigerate for half hour.

PUMPKIN SALAD

2 cups grated PUMPKIN

1 or 2 sweet APPLES, cored, cut julienne style

1 1/2 cups thinly sliced SAVOY CABBAGE

1/2 cup chopped WALNUTS

CASHEW DRESSING*

Cut pumpkin in eights from top to bottom. Remove seeds. Peel. Toss first four ingredients together. pour dressing over top.

RAW BEET SALAD

2 medium BEETS, peeled, cut julienne style

1 small KOHLRABI, peeled, grated

1 cup ALFALFA SPROUTS, cut in half

1/3 cup chopped WALNUTS

1 medium CUCUMBER, chopped

2 tablespoons "Mild" LIQUID SOY

SALAD GREENS

1/4 cup chopped BLACK OLIVES (optional)

1/4 cup SUNFLOWER SEEDS

Combine first four ingredients. Cover and refrigerate. Put soy and cucumber in blender and liquefy. Prepare a bed of greens. Scoop mixture on greens. Pour dressing over top. Garnish with sunflower seeds and olives. Serves two.

RED CABBAGE & CORN

RED CABBAGE for two, shredded

2 cups SUNFLOWER SPROUTS

1 CUCUMBER, sliced

2 ears CORN, kerneled

1/2 teaspoon CARAWAY SEED

TOMATILLO CUCUMBER DRESSING*

2 tablespoons chopped OLIVES

Mix cabbage and sprouts. Spread on plate leaving 1" around the edge. Sprinkle on caraway. Place cucumber slices around the outer edge of plate. Note: If using organic cucumber, it is not necessary to peel. Spoon the corn in a circle next to cucumbers. Pour dressing over top. Garnish with chopped olives in center. Serves two.

RED CABBAGE & PARSNIPS

RED CABBAGE for 2, shredded

2 PARSNIPS, grated

1 cup fresh PEAS

1/2 cup PINE NUTS (optional)

1 cup ALFALFA SPROUTS, cut in half

2 or 3 fresh OREGANO LEAVES, minced

1 medium CUCUMBER, chopped

2 tablespoons "Mild" LIQUID SOY

1/3 cup sliced OLIVES

Combine first six ingredients on dinner plate. Place soy and cucumber in blender and liquefy. Pour dressing over top. Garnish with olives.

RUTABAGA, KALE & BOK CHOY

1 medium RUTABAGA, grated

1 or 2 stalks BOK CHOY, cut in half length-wise, slivered diagonally

1 ear of CORN, kerneled

1/2 teaspoon CARAWAY SEED

CREAMY CELERY DRESSING*

1 small bunch KALE, chopped, steamed 2 minutes
 (See "How to Steam" on page 12).

1/4 cup chopped OLIVES

Steam kale after other foods are prepared. Combine rutabaga, bok choy, corn, and caraway. Prepare dressing. Steam kale. Combine kale with first four ingredients. Place on dinner plate. Pour dressing over top. Garnish with olives. Serves two.

SNOW PEAS & ZUCCHINI

2 medium ZUCCHINI, grated

1 ear of CORN, kerneled

3/4 cup diced CHERRY TOMATOES

1 cup ALFALFA SPROUTS, cut in half

1/2 teaspoon DILL SEED

CREAMY CELERY DRESSING*

Handful SNOW PEAS

SALAD GREENS

Pitted BLACK OLIVES

Combine first five ingredients. Scoop onto bed of greens. Peel stem and string off snow peas. Place in a pinwheel design on plate. Place olives between spokes. Pour dressing over top. Serves two.

"SPAGHETTI, TOMATO SAUCE & CHEESE"*

Grated SPAGHETTI SQUASH for two

3/4 pound ripe TOMATOES, quartered

1 small GARLIC CLOVE, diced

Fresh PARSLEY and SWEET BASIL, minced

1/2 cup Pre-soaked GARBANZO BEANS (See "How to .." on page 12).

Rinse and drain garbanzo beans. Cut squash in half at center. Remove seeds. Refrigerate half for other use. Slice squash in thirds. Easier to peel when sliced. Peel or cut off skin. Grate in a food processor. Refrigerate in covered bowl. Put tomatoes and garlic in electric blender and liquefy. Use fine grater for garbanzo beans. Put squash on plate. Pour tomato over it. Sprinkle on parsley and sweet basil. Sprinkle garbanzo "cheese" on top. Serve with a small green salad or on a bed of spinach. Serves two.

*Note: This dish requires soaking of garbanzo beans for two days.

SPINACH, BRUSSELS SPROUTS & CORN

1/2 bunch SPINACH (see "How To Prepare Spinach" on page 12)

4 to 6 BRUSSELS SPROUTS, sliced thin. Separate layers.

2 ears of CORN, kerneled

1 large CARROT, grated

1 tablespoon fresh minced OREGANO

CREAMY TOMATO DRESSING*

1/3 cup sliced OLIVES

Break spinach in bite-size pieces. Combine with next four ingredients. Refrigerate while preparing dressing. Pour dressing over top. Garnish with olives. Serves two.

SPINACH & JERUSALEM ARTICHOKE

SPINACH for two (see "How to Wash" on page 12)

1 RED PEPPER, diced

1 YELLOW PEPPER, diced

TOMATILLO CUCUMBER DRESSING*

1/2 cup sliced BLACK OLIVES

Break spinach into bite-size pieces. Scrub artichokes well. Slice thin. Combine first four ingredients. Pour dressing over top. Garnish with olives.

SPINACH, BARLEY & BEETS*

Small bunch SPINACH, (see "How To Wash" on page 12).

1 cup uncooked BARLEY

1 1/2 cups DISTILLED WATER

1 cup julienned BEETS

1 cup ALFALFA SPROUTS, cut in half

2 tablespoons finely grated DAIKON (optional)

1/2 teaspoon DILL SEED

CREAMY CUCUMBER DRESSING*

1/3 cup BLACK OLIVES

Use distilled water to soak barley. When preparing meal, rinse barley and drain well. Combine spinach, barley, beets, sprouts, daikon, and dill. Pour dressing over top. Garnish with olives. Serves two.

*Note: This recipe requires soaking of barley night before.

SQUASH ITALIANO

2 medium size ZUCCHINI, grated

1 small YELLOW or GREEN BELL PEPPER, diced

3/4 cup fresh PEAS

3 or 4 PLUM TOMATOES, chopped small

1 1/2 cups ALFALFA, cut in half

2 tablespoons mild SALSA

1 tablespoon fresh, minced BASIL LEAVES

AVOCADO TOMATILLO DRESSING*

1/2 cup sliced OLIVES

Mix first seven ingredients well. Chill if desired. Pour dressing over top. Garnish with olives. Serves two.

STUFFED CHARD LEAVES

6 large SWISS CHARD leaves

2 medium-small ZUCCHINI, grated

2 ears of CORN, kerneled

1/2 cup diced tender center of CELERY

4 PLUM TOMATOES, diced

1 cup ALFALFA SPROUTS, cut in half

2 fresh BASIL LEAVES, minced

CREAMY TOMATO DRESSING*

1/2 cup chopped OLIVES

Steam chard for 2 minutes. Follow instructions under "How to Steam" on page 12. Combine next six ingredients. Determine equal portions by separating mixture on a platter. Score raised side of stem on chard so it will roll. Scoop mixture on chard. Roll from stem end. Hold with a toothpick. Pour dressing over top. Garnish with chopped olives. Serves two.

STUFFED GRAPE LEAVES*

1/4 cup pre-soaked CURRANTS

1 ear of CORN, kerneled

1 cup uncooked BARLEY

1 1/2 cups DISTILLED WATER

1 sprig PARSLEY, chopped

1/4 cup PINE NUTS

1 medium CARROT, grated

6 fresh or bottled GRAPE LEAVES

CASHEW DRESSING*

Tender stalks of CELERY, sliced lengthwise, cut 3" long

*This dish requires soaking barley overnight.

Use distilled water and soak barley overnight. When preparing meal, drain well. Combine currants, corn barley, parsley, pine nuts, and carrot.

If using bottled grape leaves, scald with 2 cups hot water and drain into a collander. If you have never used bottled grape leaves before, they are tightly rolled up in one roll, and pushed snugly in a bottle. Use tongs to get them out. A few might be damaged but there's more than enough to use. If using fresh leaves, drop young pale-green leaves into boiling water and blanch till color darkens–about 4 to 5 minutes. Drain on a rack. Cut off stems of either fresh or canned leaves. Pat dry with clean cloth dish towel. Put shiny surface down on cloth towel. Use a spoon and set the stuffing near the broad end of the leaf and fold over the left and right segments. Then roll the enclosed ball toward the leaf-tip. Place on individual plates. Pour dressing over top. Accompany dish with celery sticks. Serves two.

STUFFED PEPPERS with BARLEY*

2 large green BELL PEPPERS

1 cup uncooked BARLEY

1 ear CORN, kerneled

1/2 cup PEAS

2 PLUM TOMATOES, diced

2 large TOMATOES, chopped

3 fresh OREGANO LEAVES, minced

Soak barley in 1 1/2 cups distilled water overnight. Green pepper is difficult to digest because it is not fully ripe. A red pepper is simply a green pepper that has been left on the bush to ripen. If you prefer to cook green peppers, three minutes in the steamer is all that is necessary. Slice pepper from top to bottom. Remove seeds but don't cut off stem section. Rinse barley with hot water. Drain well. Combine with corn and peas and tomato. Puree tomatoes and oregano in electric blender. Add six tablespoons to mixture to moisten. Scoop into peppers. Pour rest of dressing over peppers. Serves two.

*Note: This recipe requires soaking barley overnight.

STUFFED PEPPERS with JICAMA

2 large GREEN BELL PEPPERS

1 cup grated JICAMA

1 ear CORN, kerneled

2 PLUM TOMATOES, diced

1 teaspoon CUMIN SEED

CrREAMY TOMATO DRESSING*

bed of GREENS

Cut peppers in half from bottom to top. Leave stem on. Remove seeds. If you prefer to cook green peppers, steam only 3 minutes. Combine jicama, corn, tomatoes, cumin seed, and 6 tablespoons of the dressing. Spoon into peppers. Pour dressing over top. Serve peppers on a bed of lettuce or sprouts.

STUFFED PEPPERS with ZUCCHINI

2 large RED BELL PEPPERS

2 medium ZUCCHINI, grated

1/3 cup PINE NUTS

2 BRUSSELS SPROUTS, sliced thin, separated from layers

1/3 cup SLICED OLIVES

ALFALFA SPROUTS

CASHEW DRESSING*

If you prefer to cook peppers, cut peppers in half lengthwise and seed. Steam 3 minutes. Don't cut away stem section. Combine next four ingredients. Add six tablespoons dressing to mixture to moisten. Scoop into peppers. Put peppers on a bed of alfalfa sprouts. Pour rest of dressing over peppers. Serves two.

STUFFED TOMATOES

4 medium size TOMATOES

1/2 cup PEAS

1 small ZUCCHINI, grated

1 ear of CORN, kerneled

1 HAAS AVOCADO

2 tablespoons "Mild" LIQUID SOY

BOSTON LETTUCE

6 pitted large BLACK OLIVES

Cut stem from tomatoes. Cut in eighths not quite to the bottom. Refrigerate. Combine next three ingredients. Refrigerate. Cut avocado in half. Remove pit. Cut thin slices in both directions while still in skin. Scoop pulp out with tablespoon. Put avocado and soy in small bowl. Soften by smashing with fork. Blend avocado in mixture. Place tomato on bed of lettuce. Scoop mixture into center and spaces between tomato wedges. Garnish with olives. Serves two.

THREE-BEAN SALAD*

1 /3 cup DRY GARBANZO BEANS ("See How to Soak" on page 12).

1/2 cup DRY KIDNEY BEANS

Large handful STRING BEANS

3 cups DRINKING WATER

1 large TOMATILLO, chopped

2 tablespoons finely grated fresh GINGER

1 tablespoon DILL SEED

2 tablespoons fresh, minced OREGANO LEAVES

1 medium TOMATILLO, diced

1/2 medium CUCUMBER, grated (can leave skin on if organic).

2 cups SUNFLOWER SPROUTS

Use large tomatillo in marinate. If you have a nut chopper liquefy it. A tomato press is also effective. If neither of these are available, dice it finely. Put tomatillo, ginger, dill, and oregano in water. Remove stem and string from string beans. Cut diagonally in bite-size pieces. Place garbanzos, kidney beans and string beans in a covered casserole dish. Pour marinate over top. Mix beans again in the morning. Soak for two days, mixing occasionally. (Not all the kidney beans will swell. Remove all small, bright red kidney beans before serving).

To prepare for meal: Transfer to pot. Bring to a boil. Turn off heat immediately. Leave on hot grate for 15 minutes. Return beans in casserole dish by using a wide-hole serving spoon. Remove any large pieces of ginger and seasoning. Mix second tomatillo and cucumber together. Add to beans and mix. Scoop on bed of sunflower sprouts,

*Note: This recipe requires marinating for two days.

VEGE BURGERS

2 cups CARROT PULP left over from juicing

3/4 cup ground SUNFLOWER SEEDS

1/2 cup diced CELERY

3 tablespoons DAIKON, minced

2 tablespoons "Mild" LIQUID SOY

4 tablespoons BRAGGS BOUILLON

1 cup finely chopped ZUCCHINI

SALAD GREENS

MEXICAN SALSA*

Mix first four ingredients. Add soy, bouillon and zucchini. Mix and knead well. Form into patties. Serve on a bed of greens. Spoon salsa over top.

YAM & APPLE SALAD

2 cups grated YAMS

2 yellow-skinned APPLES, seeded, cut in small cubes

1/2 cup grated JICAMA

1 cup ALFALFA SPROUTS, cut in half

1 teaspoon ANISE

1 cup fresh APPLE JUICE

1/3 cup SUNFLOWER SEEDS

BOSTON LETTUCE

1/2 cup RAISINS (pre-soaked over night, or pour boiling water over top,

    and let stand while preparing dish).

As you are preparing the first three ingredients, put them in a bowl with apple juice to prevent discoloration. When ready to complete dish, drain well and save apple juice. Toss in alfalfa sprouts and anise. Put remaining apple juice (need 3/4 cup), and sunflower seeds in blender and blend until smooth. Scoop mixture over a bed of greens. Pour dressing on top. Sprinkle with raisins. Serves two.

YAMS & SAVOY CABBAGE

2 cups grated YAMS

1 cup thinly sliced SAVOY CABBAGE

1 ear CORN, kerneled

1 teaspoon ANISE

1/3 pound SNOW PEAS, remove stem and peel string off

CASHEW DRESSING*

Prepare dressing first. Grate yams last to lessen discoloration time. Combine first four ingredients. Place snow peas on dish in a pinwheel design. Scoop mixture in center. Pour dressing over top. Serves two.

YAM & WALNUT LOAF

3/4 cup OATMEAL

1/2 cup DRINKING WATER

2 cups grated YAMS

1/2 cup chopped WALNUTS

1 ear CORN, kerneled

1/4 cup diced CELERY

SALAD GREENS

CASHEW DRESSING*

Soak oatmeal 5 minutes. Combine next four ingredients, preparing yams last to lessen discoloration time. Mix thoroughly. Form into individual loaves. Place on salad greens. Pour dressing over top. Serve immediately. Serves two.

ZUCCHINI & AVOCADOS with CARROTS

Grated ZUCCHINI or two

1 large HAGS AVOCADO

1 large CARROT, grated (need 1 cup).

2 tablespoons "Mild" LIQUID SOY

1/2 teaspoon DILL SEED (optional)

4 large ROMAINE leaves, sliced in thin strips.

Grate zucchini and carrot with a coarse grater. Cut avocado in half. Remove pit. Cut thin slices in both directions while still in skin. Remove with a tablespoon into bowl with zucchini and carrot. Sprinkle with soy and dill. Mix. Make a bed of greens with lettuce. Scoop mixture on top.

ZUCCHINI & GREEN BEANS

2 medium ZUCCHINI, grated

GREEN BEANS for two, remove stems, cut diagonally

1 small YELLOW SQUASH, chopped

1 cup ALFALFA SPROUTS

1/3 cup sliced BLACK OLIVES

CREAMY CUCUMBER DRESSING*

SALAD GREENS

Mix first four ingredients. Scoop on to bed of greens. Pour dressing on top. Garnish with olives.

ZUCCHINI, SNOW PEAS & CORN

2 cups grated ZUCCHINI

1/2 pound SNOW PEAS, cut in thirds

2 ears CORN, kerneled

3 tablespoons finely grated DAIKON

1 cup SUNFLOWER SPROUTS

2 OREGANO LEAVES, minced

TOMATILLO CUCUMBER DRESSING*

1/4 cup chopped OLIVES

SALAD GREENS

Combine first six ingredients. Scoop onto bed of greens. Pour dressing over top. Garnish with olives. Serves two.

ZUCCHINI & SPINACH SALAD

1 small bunch SPINACH (See "How To Wash.." on page 12).

2 medium-size ZUCCHINI, grated

1 ear of CORN, kerneled

(or can use YELLOW CROOK SQUASH, grated)

1 red BELL PEPPER, diced

1 cup SUNFLOWER SPROUTS, cut in half

TOMATILLO CUCUMBER DRESSING*

STUFFED GREEN OLIVES

Combine first five ingredients. Pour dressing over top. Garnish with olives. Serves two.

BIBLIOGRAPHY

<u>Fit For Life</u>
    Harvey & Marilyn Diamond
    666 Fifth Avenue
    New York, NY 10103

<u>Superior Nutrition</u>
    Dr. Herbert M. Shelton
    Willow Publishing, Inc.
    San Antonio, TX

Books by T.C. Fry:

<u>I Live On Fruit</u> (Essie Honiball, co-author)

<u>The Great Water Controversy</u>

<u>How To Keep Your Body Pure</u>

<u>Correct Food Combining For Easy Digestion</u> (Dr. Herbert Shelton, co-author)

Health Excellence Systems
    1108 Regal Row
    Manchaca, Texas 78652-60609

The Health Reporter
    (Series of 20 Volumes)
    Health Excellence Systems
    1108 Regal Row
    Manchaca, TX 78652

<u>The Greengrocer</u>
    by Joe Carcione
    Chronicle Books
    275 5th Street
    San Francisco, CA 94103

Jean Anderson Cooks
Wilhan Morrow & Co., Inc.
105 Madison Avenue
New York, NY 10016

Nontoxic & Natural
by Debra Lynn Dadd
Nontoxic Lifestyles, Inc
P. 0. Box 210019
San Francisco, CA 94121-0019

The Health Seekers' Yearbook: A Revolutionist's Handbook for Getting Well & Staying Well Without The Medicine Men
by Victoria Bidwell
Get Well*Stay Well, America!
1776 Hygiene Joy Way
Mt. Vernon, WA 98273
(206) 428-3687

RECOMMENDED READING

The Christ Diet
by Charles J. Hunt III
Heartquake Publishing
P.O. Box 593
La Jolla, CA 92038

Blatant Raw Food Propaganda!
By Joe Alexander
Blue Dolphin Publishing, Inc.
PO Box 1908
Nevada City, CA 95959

Original Diet: Raw Vegetarian Guide and Recipe Book
by Karen Cross Whyte
Troubador Press
385 Fremont
San Francisco, CA 94105

Raw Energy
by Leslie and Susannah Kenton
Warner Books, Inc.
666 Fifth Avenue
New York, NY 10103

The Uncook Book: Raw Food Adventures To A New Health High
>by Elizabeth & Dr. Elton Baker
Communication Creativity
433 Fourth Street
P. O. Box 213
Saguache, CO 81149

Why Christians Get Sick
>by Rev. George H. Malkmus
Hallelujah Acres Publishing
Eidson, Tennessee 37731

Books by Harvey & Marilyn Diamond:

Fit for Life

A New Way of Eating

Living Health
>Warner Books, Inc.
666 Fifth Avenue
New York, NY 10103

Your Heart Your Planet
>Harvey Diamond
Hay House, Inc.
501 Santa Monica Boulevard
Santa Monica, CA 90406

Light Eating for Survival
>Marcia Madhuri Acciardo
21st Century Publications
P.O. Box 702
Fairfield, IA 52556

Dick Gregory's Natural Diet for Folks Who Eat: Cookin' with Mother Nature
>Perennial Library
Harper & Row, Publishers
New York

RAW LEARNING

Phyllis Avery's Raw Food Preparation Classes

> Hygeia Publishing
> 1358 Fern Way
> Vista, CA 92083

Ann Wigmore Institute
Workshops in raw food preparation.
196 Commonwealth Ave.
Boston, Mass. 02116
(617)267-9424

Sylvia Green Living Foods Workshops
Los Angeles, California
(310) 399-5612

The Optimum Health Institute
A residential facility offering raw food preparation.
6970 Central Ave,
Lemon Grove, CA 91945
(619) 464-3346

Bodhi Tree Bookstore
8585 Melrose Ave.
West Hollywood, CA 90069
(310) 659-1733

JUICE BARS AND RESTAURANTS

Beverly Hills Juice Club
8382 Beverly Blvd.
LOS Angeles, CA
(213) 655-8300

Cafe La De Da
2010 Jimmy Durante Boulevard
Del Mar, CA
(619) 792-2221 (Open for lunch and
dinner only. Call for hours.)

Garden Taste
1555 Camino Del Mar
(in the Del Mar Plaza)
Del Mar, California
(619) 793-1500

Get Juiced
1423 Fifth St.
Santa Monica, CA
(213) 395-8177

Govinda's Natural Foods Restaurant
3102 University Avenue
San Diego, CA
(619) 284-4826

I Love Juicy
7174 Melrose Ave.
Los Angeles, CA
(213) 935-7247
&
10845 Lindbrook Drive
Westwood, CA (310) 208-3242
&

Hampton Drive
Venice, CA
(310) 399-1318

Fountain Of Juice
1163 First St.
Encinitas, CA
(619) 944-0612

Ki's Juice Bar
206 Birmingham Drive
Cardiff by the Sea, CA
(619) 436-5236

La Hood's Natural Juices
Grand Central Market
317 S. Broadway
Los Angeles, CA
(213) 629-2787

The Vegetarian
431 W. 13th Avenue
Escondido, CA
(619) 740-9596

NATURAL HYGIENE ORGANIZATIONS

THE AMERICAN NATURAL HYGIENE SOCIETY
P.O. Box 30630
Tampa, FL 33630
(818) 855-6607

THE CANADIAN NATURAL HYGIENE SOCIETY
Attn: Joe Aaron
P.O. Box 235, Station "T"
Toronto, Ontario, Canada M6B 4A1

GET WELL STAY WELL, AMERICA!
Attn: Victoria Bidwell*
1776 The Hygiene Joy Way
Mt. Vernon, WA 98273
(206) 428-3687

HEALTH EXCELLENCE SYSTEMS
Attn: T.C. Fry
1108 Regal Row
Manchaca, TX 78652
(512) 280-5566

NATURAL HYGIENE, INCORPORATED
Attn: Jo Willard
P.O. Box 2132
Huntington, CT 06084
(203) 929-1557

*Write to Victoria for a list of natural hygiene doctors in the United States.
Please include a self-addressed, stamped envelope.

****

ORDER SHEET

THE GARDEN OF EDEN RAW FRUIT & VEGETABLE RECIPES - 120 pages ($10.95)
All vegan - no milk products.
Fruit Recipes - Hors D'Oeuvres, Fruit Dishes, Fruit Syrups, Fruit Shakes and Fruit Drinks.
Vegetable Recipes - Soups, Dips, Dressing (made from fresh vegetables - no vinegar, oil or mayonnaise), and Main Dishes.

THE 10-MINUTE VEGETARIAN COOK BOOK - 144 pages ($11.95)
All main dish recipes calling for fresh vegetables. All meals cook in 10 minutes or less.
Minimal use of processed foods.

STOP YOUR TINNITUS: Causes, Preventatives, Treatments ($14.95)
184 page book offers: External Causative Agents, Chemicals, Internal Causative Disorders, Physiological Intervention, Psychological Intervention, Alimentary Intervention, Telephone Hearing Screening Test, 13 pages of Glossary terms, 16 pages of Resources, 108 Medical and Scientific References.

The book shares the experiences of nine people from a Tinnitus Self-Help Group with the modalities that helped them stop their tinnitus.

Add $1.75 shipping for 1 book. $2.00 for 2 or 3. When shipped to California, add 8% sales tax. Please allow 3 to 4 weeks for delivery.

Order From:

Phyllis Avery
c/o Hygeia Publishing
1358 Fern Place
Vista, CA 92083